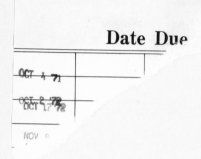

MINISTERING
TO DEEPLY
TROUBLED PEOPLE

SUCCESSFUL PASTORAL COUNSELING SERIES

MINISTERING
TO DEEPLY
TROUBLED PEOPLE

ERNEST E. BRUDER

PRENTICE-HALL, INC., ENGLEWOOD CLIFFS, N.J.

Ministering to Deeply Troubled People
by Ernest E. Bruder

© 1963 by Prentice-Hall, Inc., Library of Congress Catalog
Card Number: 63–18120. All rights reserved, including the
right to reproduce this book or any portions thereof, in any
form, except for the inclusion of brief quotations in a review.

T—58424

Prentice-Hall International, Inc.
(*London, Tokyo, Sydney, Paris*)
Prentice-Hall of Canada, Ltd.
Prentice-Hall de Mexico, S.A.

Printed in the United States of America

DEDICATION

To those deeply troubled people
—especially one—
who during my eighteen years at
Saint Elizabeths Hospital,
in trusting and sharing of
themselves as they really are,
have helped me find the courage to do the same.

ACKNOWLEDGMENTS

Grateful acknowledgment is made for permission to use material previously published in part in *Pastoral Psychology* and *The Journal of Pastoral Care,* and to Atlantic–Little, Brown and Company for permission to reproduce part of Brian Moore's *The Lonely Passion of Judith Hearne.*

I want to thank Captain (U.S.N. ret.) and Mrs. Philip Wakeman for their many helpful and constructive editorial criticisms while the manuscript was in preparation. For expert and painstaking secretarial and editorial assistance much credit is due to Miss Eleanor Hanshew, Mr. Philip Rickert, Miss Marian Klein, Mrs. Beatrice Swoyer and Mr. Earl O. Coon.

In one of the most important acknowledgments I would like to make, I am stopped by the stigma which, even in this supposedly enlightened day, still attaches to mental illness. The reader will note in the footnotes in Chapter One and in the passage in Chapter Four, that mental hospital patients have collaborated in the writing of this book. I know of no other published work where this privilege has been made available to an author, and in so helpful a way. I would particularly like to acknowledge by name my debt to one of our patients—a very gifted and sensitive young woman. Yet to do so would be to expose her to possible injury from those who do not—are so afraid to—understand. So my best teachers must remain anonymous. This is a measure of how far we still have to go in understanding mental illness. It is, in fact, a measure of how far we still have to go in allowing the teachings of Our Lord to become more than just a verbal part of our daily living.

Ernest E. Bruder

INTRODUCTION

This series of books represents the most comprehensive publishing effort ever made in the field of pastoral care. These books could not have been published twenty-five years ago, or probably even ten, for the material was not then available. In the past, single books have been available covering different phases of the task. Now we are bringing the subjects together in a single series. Here we present a library of pastoral care covering the major topics and problems that most pastors will encounter in their ministry. Fortunately, not all of these problems need be faced every week or even every month. But, when they are, the minister wants help and he wants it immediately.

These books are prepared for the nonspecialized minister serving the local church, where he is the most accessible professional person in the community. It is a well-accepted fact that more people turn to clergy when in trouble than to all other professional people. Therefore, the pastor must not fail them.

Russell L. Dicks
General Editor

Someone will come then, watch and see
Be concerned for me and care
My life left but in minutes
And death before me bare.
Oh bitterness too late for tears
My soul within tried sore—
Please go, I do not need you now
I needed you before.

—a mental patient
Saint Elizabeths Hospital

FOREWORD

Ever since Anton T. Boisen began his pioneer work at the Worcester, Massachusetts, State Hospital nearly two score years ago, there has been a steadily widening recognition of the value of clinical training for the clergy. It is to the clergyman that the majority of troubled people first turn for advice and assistance; what more logical, then, that he should have a working knowledge of the mental mechanisms of the men and women who appeal to him for help?

As William James pointed out sixty years ago, in his masterly volume *The Varieties of Religious Experience,* the mental hospital is *the* place, indeed almost the only place, where mental mechanisms may be studied intimately, "unmasked by their usual surroundings." It is for this reason that the resources of the mental hospital have been utilized in the clinical pastoral-training programs. Not only have their programs brought religious ministrations to the patients in these hospitals, but they have demonstrated to the seminarians and clergy under training the truth that mental patients are people, too, and that they differ only in degree from the individuals with whom the clergyman and, indeed, the rest of us, too, rub shoulders in our day-to-day contacts.

One very effective program of this sort has been developed since 1944 at Saint Elizabeths Hospital in Washington, D.C., under the energetic and far-sighted leadership of the author of the present volume, Chaplain Ernest E. Bruder. The book is no armchair or doctrinaire presentation. It gives us the distillation of nearly twenty years of actual and progressive experience in training theology students, chaplain interns and residents and community clergy—yes, and in bringing to the medical staff an appreciation of the benefits of religion in psychiatric work.

What follows, then, is practical, and is presented cogently, both as to the *raison d'être* of clinical training of the clergy and as to its actual practice. It is a volume which can be read with profit by all who teach and practice in the field of the pastoral ministry.

Winfred Overholser, M.D., Sc.D.,
Superintendent, Saint Elizabeths Hospital, 1937–1962,
Past President, American Psychiatric Association

CONTENTS

CONTENTS

PREFACE

PREFACE

I want to begin this book by trying to answer some basic questions. If this at least is attempted, then the reader has some idea of what to expect. In a field where all feel themselves expert—human relations—and where there still remains so much confusion and uncertainty, it is well to take very little for granted.

How did this book come to be written? For a number of years, as a result of clinical pastoral teaching and chaplain concerns in a large federal mental hospital, I have increasingly felt the need to struggle with, organize and expand some of the understandings developed during more than 20 years of experience in working with deeply troubled people.[1]

Writing this book was not an easy task. Something constantly kept getting in my way. At long last I think I was able to identify the block. My thought had been to write an entirely new book. I had already written considerable about this ministry and some of my writing had already been published, though only in separate papers and with limited circulation. Finally I realized that all this material demanded reorganization. It was not until this became clear and I began reworking both published and unpublished material, that the book began to take shape. New sections and emphases were added to bring the work closer to its title and object—to give some clear understanding of what a ministry to deeply troubled people is and how it is carried out.

For whom is this volume intended? Quite simply, it is intended for the busy pastor. He was the one I had in mind as this material was rethought and reworked. The busy pastor—conscientiously,

---

[1] The views expressed in this book are those of the author and not necessarily those of the Department of Health, Education and Welfare.

hopefully going about his work with often only the most unclear idea of what he is about. The busy pastor—about whom much has recently been written to indicate that far more is expected from him than is humanly possible, or even advisable. The busy pastor—who so often has been graduated from an accredited seminary, full of enthusiasm and high ideals, only to have found within the first five years of his ministry that he has become very confused by the constant and varied problems of his people.

But, he remains the busy pastor! His is still the ministry to which he has been called; his situation has not changed. He has only become more acutely aware of his dilemma. He has been ordained with the word that gives life and has joyously embraced the ministry of reconciliation, yet he frequently has become little more than a machine going about his offices. It is no wonder that of late the question has been asked frequently by ministers and lay people alike: Are ministers more prone to mental illness than members of other professions? For what it is worth, I draw attention to the fact that nobody can really answer that question, though there have been published some very ill-advised and exceedingly poor "research" studies which would have us believe this to be true. From 20 years of work in mental hospitals and from my experience in teaching both seminarians and clergymen, it is my strong impression that clergymen are no more vulnerable to mental illness than any other professional group. However, this should not be interpreted as meaning that some do not have very serious personal and professional concerns. This will be dealt with more extensively.

The book, then, is primarily intended for the busy pastor who wants to help the deeply troubled people who are his charge. He is frequently bewildered by what he knows is going on all around him but which eludes him because he cannot give it clear definition. Yet, it is to this busy pastor that some 42 per cent of all people who seek aid in solving their "difficulties in living"[2] first turn for help.[3] He knows from painful experience that they will often not gain from

[2] A very descriptive phrase often used by the American psychiatrist, Dr. Harry Stack Sullivan.
[3] Joint Commission on Mental Health and Illness, *Action for Mental Health* (New York: Basic Books, 1961), p. 103.

him the help they so desperately need. Also, a majority of pastors have admitted that they are not spending as much time counseling as their own recognition of the need would indicate.[4] The pastor intends to help, and he can marshal an incredible number of hours and days per week to prove he is actively concerned and engaged in the Lord's work. But, honest as he is, he will be the first to admit, if given the opportunity with no condemnation, that he is bewildered and sick about the whole business—even while his people are declaring his success!

The busy pastor, going about his regular rounds of parish and pastoral calling, visiting and counseling, before, during and after troubles become acute, is deeply concerned about doing his work more helpfully. He tries to anticipate trouble, he seeks to be a support during trouble and, when lives are shattered, he helps to pick up the pieces. He wants to understand more of what his people have experienced and are experiencing to make them behave as they do. He knows that he has so much to learn, and hasn't given up trying. He anticipates longingly that "it is better to minister unto others than to be ministered to" but has not yet found the strength and meaning he knows are contained in these words. It is to him I speak.

Now, about whom is the book written? Is it about the approximately 750,000 deeply troubled people who occupy over half the beds in *all* our hospitals today? No, though the busy pastor must include these as part of his regular pastoral ministry, for they have been far too long neglected in the regular pastoral functions.

This book is really about the 18,000,000 people the Surgeon General of the United States estimates are in serious need of concerned and expert help with their daily living—so much in need that one often wonders whether they should not be in a hospital—if not for their own good, perhaps for the sake of those around them. It is from this group that so many of the demands made upon the busy pastor come, and it is from this group that he so often retreats, defeated and uncomprehending.

In a sense this book is about all deeply troubled people and for

---

[4] Richard McCann, *The Churches and Mental Health* (New York: Basic Books, 1962), pp. 69 ff.

all deeply troubled people. From the pastor's point of view in the exercise of his religious and pastoral functions it does not matter whether they are in or out of the hospital. What makes the situation more complicated is that the more deeply troubled people are often scarcely aware of the fact, and it is, therefore, more dangerous to try and meet the evidences of their difficulties head-on.

I will attempt to articulate the understandings I have reached about some basic concerns and issues, which have made clearer my own ministry to deeply troubled people. That these understandings were gained as a result of a ministry largely to those who were mentally ill and in hospitals is no accident. As William James has so eloquently testified,[5] it is much easier to identify and study a complicated process when it is exaggerated. Symptoms of mental illness are often an exaggeration or distortion of regular patterns of behavior. I must emphasize that when the mentally ill are regarded as "very much like ourselves, only more so"[6] then it becomes necessary and unavoidable to contend with and resolve the issues which arise from admitting the truth of this observation. This is, of course, so much easier said than done. When attempted, this sometimes comes off so badly that one remains as confused as ever, though temporarily lulled into a sense of false security *by the sound of acceptable words.*[7] Much more will have to be said about this in the pages dealing with mental illness and the meaning of anxiety. Here it should suffice to alert the reader to the fact that mental illness is largely viewed by this author as a distortion in our inter-relatedness. It cannot ever really be understood in terms of its origins and cure apart from our recognizing the varying ways we ourselves are involved in and con-

---

[5] William James, *The Varieties of Religious Experience* (New York: The Modern Library (Random House), first published 1902), p. 23.

[6] Dr. Winfred Overholser, superintendent at Saint Elizabeths Hospital, Washington, D.C., 1937–1962, and formerly president of the American Psychiatric Association, frequently used this phrase in his lectures.

[7] I have reference here to those writers in the field of human relations who have espoused the term "interpersonal relations," but who betray in their writings the lack of any real understanding of the concept. This is an area in which Dr. Harry Stack Sullivan did a good deal of serious investigation. He gave the term "interpersonal relations" a rather precise meaning. It is this meaning which has been lost to the writers in the field who have been caught up in the magic of the new sounds.

tribute to it, both negatively and positively, as friends, relatives or pastors.

Finally, a word about the author. Who is this person who thinks he has something worthwhile to say to the busy pastor? Who is this person who may, with the sound of some very plausible phrases, be offering nothing more than a neat maneuver by which the busy pastor is inveigled into buying and even *reading* another book which suggests it may have answers to some of the questions which genuinely plague him? It is a fair question, one all too frequently evaded by authors.

In a way, this answer should be attempted in a much more thorough fashion than is going to be the case. However, there will be enough clues to indicate the directions in which we will be moving together, and the unwary will have been warned. For the honest investigator willing to undertake the slow, laborious, and often painful journey of finding out what is *really* going on in this business of living together as persons (or perhaps more accurately, though somewhat cynically, *avoiding* the living together as persons) it is important that there should be some clarity about what the author has seen, said, done and learned in working quite intimately with people. What is reflected in these pages is experience-centered; and this experience is the author's living, or attempting to live, in relationship *with* others.

Out of a quite lonely and isolated life, having been graduated from a good liberal arts college and divinity school, I found myself ordained and in a small rural parish. Being large-city bred, my position did nothing to lessen either the confusion about living or the sense of isolation from people. Parish-calling was expected and faithfully carried out, but a sense of meaninglessness grew. It came to a head when, no longer having an excuse to avoid calling on a formerly active parishioner who had suddenly stopped attending church right after his wife died, I found him most responsive to my call. He even volunteered that he was going to return to church, but he never did. Neither the parishioner nor I then saw a clue as to what was needed.

Appropriately, at just this time opportunity presented itself for a year of clinical pastoral training. I had heard something about this approach during seminary days: that it was intended to help the pastor gain some understanding of what people were like, what some of their essential concerns actually were and what might be done for them pastorally. That did it!

In a way, clinical training opened a new world: It made inevitable the very kinds of interpersonal encounters for which serious students of human relations constantly seek, and which I had just as constantly managed to avoid finding. When one finds himself a minister in a mental hospital with people who have almost exhausted their seemingly endless ways of avoiding living, who are perplexed by the questions of ultimate concern (faith, hope, love, meaning, conviction, commitment, communion—the areas in which religion has found its ground for being), it simply ends as either "put up or shut up!" Here I was confronted with the basics in human living, and was forced to think through what is of fundamental concern. I was forced to establish assumptions which had relevance to the situation in which I found myself as a minister. Out of this clinical experience, then, came those basic assumptions on which both my religious ministry and my clinical teaching were predicated, and which undergird the entire substance of this book.

As a result of one full year of clinical experience in a general and a mental hospital, as well as in a prison, moving into a full-time chaplain position became inevitable. My work as a chaplain began at Norristown State Hospital in Pennsylvania in 1942 under the kindly and clinically sensitive guidance of Dr. Arthur P. Noyes.[8] It reached its fruition in the years after 1944 when I organized the first full-time clinically trained Protestant chaplain program at Saint Elizabeths Hospital, Washington, D.C., in this internationally known treatment, teaching and research center, where so much and such constant encouragement and support were given me by Dr. Winfred Overholser as superintendent.

The interpersonal confrontations unavoidable in a meaningful pastoral and teaching ministry in a mental hospital aroused anxieties which literally drove me into psychoanalysis. Here The Washington

---

[8] Now retired. The author of *Modern Clinical Psychiatry* and former president of the American Psychiatric Association.

School of Psychiatry made a much needed and most welcome contribution. Though I had already made an extensive beginning in psychoanalysis while in Philadelphia, I found the emphasis in The Washington School much more meaningful. The very first lines in the foreword of the 1944 catalogue of The Washington School caught my eye: "The Fellows of The School hold that no person may be entrusted with responsibility for therapeutic intervention in difficulties in living who shall not have undergone a searching scrutiny of his personal history, liabilities and assets from the therapeutic standpoint. In view of this basic premise in all training programs in The School, emphasis is laid on individual psychiatric counseling, taking into consideration the needs of the respective candidates in relation to the fields in which they seek training."[9]

I immediately enrolled in The School where, of course, they were curious as to why a minister should want to study psychiatry. My answer appeared to make sense to them: that I had found this discipline had much to contribute toward illuminating my own functions in working with people's difficulties in living. Later I was again to pick up my work in psychoanalysis, and in 1948 had the privilege of receiving The School's first Certificate in Applied Psychiatry for Ministers from Dr. Sullivan himself. Then for some years I served as a faculty member and am now on the Board of Directors of The Washington School of Psychiatry.

As part of the experiences which led to the writing of this book, recognition should be given to my part-time teaching at the Philadelphia Divinity School, The Virginia Theological Seminary, Howard School of Religion and the Advanced Studies School of the Washington Council of Churches, National Capital Area, in addition to a faculty position in 1947 at Westminster Theological Seminary (now Wesley Theological Seminary) which culminated in the March 1962 appointment as Howard Chandler Robbins Professor of Clinical Pastoral Care. All these experiences materially contributed to shape my formulation of basic insights and assumptions.

The people most influential in all these years are really too numerous to mention. Obviously one cannot pay tribute to all, but I

---

[9] The Washington School of Psychiatry Bulletin #9, 1944–1945.

should like to name at least some people without whom really nothing like this book would ever have been possible.

Here I must acknowledge a very profound sense of gratitude, which is far easier to write than to speak, to Ruth, my wife, and to our four children, who, perhaps better than anybody except my analyst, know me for what I am and manage to put up with me! That, for the last several years, has been an achievement of no small significance! Then there is Dr. Edith Weigert, an analyst of rare sensitivity, profound compassion, deep insight and maddening love and patience. I must mention Canon E.A.W. Gill at Saint John's College, who made it impossible for me to escape the ministry; Dr. Anton T. Boisen, chaplain emeritus at Elgin State Hospital and founder of the modern clinical pastoral training movement, who helped me regain a sense of meaning in the ministry; Robert E. Brinkman, my first clinical training supervisor, who got through to me as a person; the many, though particularly one, mentally ill patients who have been in many ways my most profound and gifted teachers; the numerous students, and Dr. Winfred Overholser, whose freely expressed interest in what I was about was a constant challenge to attempt the impossible; seminarians and clergymen alike who have challenged my formulations, and finally Mrs. Howard Chandler Robbins, who has that rare gift in her relationships of deep understanding which requires relatively little explanation concerning the complex and involved meanings of what goes on between deeply troubled people. It is to all of these particularly, and to many others as well, that I am deeply grateful for this often troublesome life and ministry.

Scientists' Cliffs
Port Republic, Maryland

MINISTERING
TO DEEPLY
TROUBLED PEOPLE

CHAPTER ONE

A PASTORAL VIEW
Of The MENTALLY ILL

Who are the mentally ill? When we ask this question in a spirit of humility before the tremendous complexities of the God-given human personality, seeking to understand something of what has happened to these people, then indeed we can learn much that will help us in our own difficulties in living.

Patients in mental hospitals *can* be our teachers. But they cannot teach those who will not hear—those who still prefer to look upon the mentally ill as subhumans who should be ostracized and isolated from the rest of the community. A colleague, chaplain in a state mental hospital, recently told me that when the question of engaging an additional chaplain for his hospital came up in the state legislature, it was voted down on the strength of the openly expressed sentiment: "What do we want another chaplain there for? They are nothing more than animals." Such is the nature of anxiety!

A New Concept of Mental Illness

However, a new understanding of the mentally ill is gradually making its way into our awareness. It is the realization that the mentally ill are people like ourselves and that they do have much to teach us. As we listen to them as teachers who have much of real value to tell us, their own shattered self-esteem is strengthened and restored. When we come to know the mentally ill, we often find them making desperate, though perhaps unwitting, attempts to shore up a low self-esteem. Low self-esteem is often the core concern in the illness itself—it is something our Lord points up in The Great Commandment, that we love ourselves.

As we dare to get close to those who are so deeply troubled, or *let them get close to us,* we hear over and over again something of the dreadful story involved in the inability to love. We learn what it means to be shut up in the prison of self so that life ends up in the farce of settling for intimacy without relationship, and the ultimate blasphemy of suffering relationships that have no intimacy. It is in just these areas that we need desperately to learn from those who have so violently protested against these indecencies. It is just here that the sanity of the insane has much to offer by way of illuminating the insanity of the sane!

Where Mental Illness Begins

There is no sharp line of division between those who are "mentally ill" and those who are "mentally healthy." For the pastor, the only meaningful and useful approach to any individual is in terms of the individual himself: *his* problems and the state of *his* health. But since we are all involved in society and our own culture, we cannot deal intelligently with emotional and mental problems or illness unless we understand what others mean when they use these terms.

The present view is that mental health is a continuum from a condition of health or wholeness at one end of the scale through varying degrees of illness or disability to extreme "sickness" at the other. The difference is of degree—quantitative rather than qualitative. In mental illness, nothing "new" has been added; there is instead a lack or a malfunctioning. If we view the spectrum of mental health as having the condition of "wholeness" at one end, next would come the lesser personality disorders or character disorders and the less disabling neuroses. After these would come the more severe personality disorders and the more serious neuroses. In all of these, although there is sickness and a lack of wholeness, the individual remains in contact, painful though it may be, with reality. Then there is a shading off into an area where there is denial and evasion of reality and it is in this ill-defined region that mental *illness* begins. As illness becomes more severe, the lack of the reality factor is more easily recognized and there is no doubt that it is mental illness. Hallucinations and delusions are often a part of this. Not only are the emotions and the factor of judgment involved, as they are in neuroses and personality disorders, the processes of logical and rational thought become involved. The senses themselves malfunction; perception of the real world is distorted. Technically, these illnesses are called *psychoses*.

The Psychoses

For purposes of diagnosis and treatment, the psychoses are divided into many categories. One major division is between those which are organic in nature and those which are functional. Organic psychoses are of many kinds, some due to congenital conditions and others the result of accident or physical injury. They range in severity from permanently and totally disabling conditions to a kind of mild, diffuse *organicity* which is difficult to identify or to pinpoint.

The majority of those who are mentally ill suffer from functional disorders, in which there may indeed be an organic factor. They might be capable of functioning mentally, however, except that the pressure of emotional and environmental factors has produced a personality unable to cope with the demands of social living. *Schizophrenia* is the major functional disorder, and this is subdivided into four types: *simple, paranoid, catatonic* and *hebephrenic*. This illness is characterized by regression—the individual who is unable to adjust to the demands of life slips back into an earlier (developmental) type of adjustment. In the hebephrenic, for example, this may go so far that the adult acts and behaves like a child of one or two years of age. Some catatonics apparently regress all the way to the womb, assuming a foetal position and becoming unresponsive to external stimulation.

For the pastor dealing daily with many different people, it is important to realize that the line between psychosis and emotional disorder is very indistinct. A person who has already crossed this hypothetical line may not exhibit the *conventional* signs of mental illness—he may continue to function in society for some time, and his difficulties may seem to be situational rather than internal. It is quite possible that some neurotics display more visible signs of inner distress than some psychotics.

The Province of the Psychiatrist

On this point, a word of warning is in order for all those who are called upon to counsel troubled people. The determination of mental illness is the province of the psychiatrist. Only someone specially trained in this field is in a position to evaluate all the factors in the case. Any professional person counseling others, however, needs to know something about the psychoses lest he continue his counseling efforts with disastrous results to the person concerned or even to himself. While it is true that few psychotics recognize their illness, some are impelled because of factors in their illness to consult the pastor in regard to what they *think* their problem is. The pastor should be alert to signs of unrealistic thinking, undue suspicion of other people, major evidence of inability to face present realities and other signs indicative of possible mental illness.

Where there is good reason to suspect the existence of a psychosis, it is clearly the duty of the pastor to attempt to refer this person to a psychiatrist. Unless there is already a good relationship of long standing between the person and his pastor, it is doubtful that a psychotic person would go to a psychiatrist just because he has been advised to do so. Generally, the neurotic is much more willing to consult a psychiatrist. Since some psychotic persons do have an awareness of their problems, they may be persuaded to go to a psychiatrist if it is pointed out to them that in these days it is not considered necessary to be mentally ill to consult a psychiatrist—that many people consult one in regard to particularly troublesome problems. The main fact which needs to be stressed here is that in such a counseling relationship, the pastor comes to the inevitable position of having to tell his parishioner, gently but firmly, that he needs more skilled help and time than the pastor is able to give. And thank God there are specialists in whom we as pastors have confidence and to whom we can refer!

If the pastor is unable to persuade the person concerned to go to a psychiatrist, he may find it necessary to consult with members of the person's family. He should, of course, *not* state that he believes that the person concerned may be psychotic. He may suspect this, but he does not know and is not qualified to judge. Instead, he should express his conviction that the person concerned is having excessive emotional difficulties, that as a pastor he lacks the knowledge and time to deal with these adequately, and that he thinks the interests of the person concerned would best be served if a psychiatrist were consulted by a member of the family in order to see what help *is* needed for this person.

While it is clearly the duty of the pastor to secure the best professional help possible for a person who is mentally ill, referral should not become a means of escaping personal responsibility. The relationship need not and should not end with the referral—the pastoral care should continue, particularly after hospitalization.[1] Following hospitalization the patient needs to have demonstrated by a pastoral visit the Church's continuing concern for him just as he is.

Likewise, referral should not become a means of avoiding the necessity of dealing personally with the problems that trouble people. Many people do not need a psychiatrist, but they do need love and understanding; they need support in bearing problems that have become too much for them; they need above all the living example of the meaning of the religious life, the knowledge that *gives* meaning to life. The question of referral will be discussed later. At this point our concern is with the responsibility of the pastor in regard to referral—a responsibility which proceeds from tender and informed concern for those unable to do for themselves.[2]

Basic Religious Assumptions

Now I will try to set forth the major assumptions which have guided me in establishing a religious ministry in the mental hospital. It has been my experience that only where one has been forced to

---

[1] Here a sensitive patient reviewing this manuscript felt moved to write me as follows: "Pastoral care that does not care while I'm *in* the hospital as well as upon my coming out, I would have nothing to do with. I know many patients who have put down their churches because they feel their churches put *them* down at the hospital-entering point. I doubt that should their pastors try to befriend them again on espying them back outside it will get much of anyplace. Fair-weather friends, after being in here, don't count."

[2] Said the patient: "Very lovely but hypocritic-sounding as the devil."

think through as clearly as possible what one is about and why one is about it, that any kind of adequate ministry can be offered the troubled person. This is the basic emphasis of clinical pastoral training: that student and supervisor alike grow increasingly in observation and understanding in the discharge of their pastoral functions. To me there has really been no other way than this to avoid falling into the category where "the blind lead the blind."

It is to be recognized, of course, that what follows is only a tentative, though important, beginning. It is my earnest hope not only to develop and clarify these basic assumptions, but that they will lead others to test them and offer their experience and understanding. In such ways a ministry to deeply troubled people can grow in meaning.

Mental illness, whatever else it is or is not, is basically a religious problem. It is like a fever, an attempt on the part of the personality at cure. It is also a desperate attempt on the part of the individual to keep from selling himself short, or being sold short as a person by his family, friends, society, culture or religion. It is an attempt to keep him from giving up those parts of himself with which he must come to terms and which are essential in his living if he is to become a whole person. Perhaps this is clearer if we consider that mental *health* means the wholeness of the individual, a working integration of what he is, what he has been and what he desires to become.

It is basic in human nature that the search for integrity takes place within the framework of the meaning of life to the individual. Mental illness is vitally involved with such "ultimates" as meaning, value, destiny, purpose, truth, reality, God, the immortal soul and salvation—we can take our choice of terminology. In working with the mentally ill one soon learns that each of these terms has come to have ambiguous, uncertain and even very confused and distorted meanings.

Integrity cannot be achieved if the person is at odds with himself, affirming in words what he denies in practice, or the reverse. In a state of severe inner conflict, he cannot know what to trust—and it is only as we can trust that we can come to believe adequately.

Mental illness, then, is involved with *faith*—faith in the Ultimate, faith in each other, faith in ourselves. Distortion and conflict in any one area affect all areas. Whether it is expressed in religious terms or not, the meaning of life, values, destiny—*ultimates*—are matters of faith and therefore are religious concerns. This is the area of the clergyman. Faith proceeds from trust and trust arises from the good relationships that we have with others.

People Who Have Been Hurt

The mentally ill are dreadfully *hurt* people. The illness shows that there is something seriously wrong in their relationships, that these have become distorted. This is especially true of the primary relationships of the family. It is no accident that many of our patients come from homes broken through lovelessness, mental illness, alcoholism, divorce, infidelity, drug addiction and crime. In their family relationships, the mentally ill have often been denied the consistency of love, affection, praise, honesty and the security for which we all hope. We find that when this security is lacking, the individual is also being denied the discipline and helpful criticism always needed for growth to maturity. Thus there is increasing evidence that mental illness in its genesis and cure must be understood as a profound commentary on what goes on and what does not go on in the human family. We are now coming to believe that little real healing of the sick can come about unless we remember that it was in the family they were hurt, and apart from the family they cannot be healed. Indeed, for the life they seek they must often find a new family—a healing community.

Usually this hurt has existed a long time. It marks a failure in certain relationships between the patient and people who are important to him, and who have not been able to give him that which makes for *life*. Quite frequently we find a lack of tenderness and warmth in the very relationships which are most demanding of these experiences. To point this up is not to blame those who have so failed our patients. Those who work with the relatives of the mentally ill soon realize how little they *chose* to be the way they are and how little they *intended* some of the things they did. Because of these failures, however, whether intentional or not, it is very important that our whole approach to those who are ill make no addition to this interpersonal hurt if we can possibly avoid it.

The mentally ill are extremely *anxious* people. In a sense, the illness itself can be regarded as a defense against *intolerable* anxiety. Not the least of the reasons why these people feel so anxious is that what has happened in their lives has seriously impaired their sense of self-esteem. We find our patients both feel and act as though they had little self-respect, and in this way the illness itself serves as a means to help them deal with some very painful feelings. As long as the individual in an acutely disturbed state is busy shouting about being God he does not have time to be aware of the fact that he is puny, mortal and scared to death.[3]

If we come to understand anxiety as "that which one experiences when one's self-esteem is threatened,"[4] much of what is being written here becomes clearer. We recognize that other people who are important in our lives expect certain things from us: that we should think in a certain way, act in a certain way, wish in a certain way, have feelings in certain ways. But when we begin to discover that we are *different*, this discovery, even though on a level outside of awareness, can provoke such intolerable pain that we experience anxiety. Need we be reminded how different from his fellows a person must feel when he grows angry and feels hatred toward others having been brought up and steeped in an environment that attempts to repudiate such feelings as the essence of badness? Growing angry is a quite normal (though very bothersome) response in human relations, but it does cut the individual off from those who are important to him. For some, this is so intolerable that the anger is never admitted to awareness and the individual tries to deny those feelings which are a part of his connection with the rest of humanity. Such inadmissible feelings are not necessarily negative; impulses

---

[3] Wrote the same patient referred to earlier: "I have found that most patients who shout about being God or some such equivalent (Ha) still believe so during the times that they should be scared to death, puny and mortal. It is not at all as obvious as you make it sound, nor as simple. And anyway every time I get to this place you sound sicker to me than they do."

[4] Dr. Harry Stack Sullivan.

toward tenderness for some reason in our culture often provoke equally intolerable anxiety and have to be denied.

In the mentally ill person, the denial and evasion of intolerable feelings common to everyone is carried to an extreme where reality itself is denied or evaded. We can easily imagine the need for such evasion if we stop to think about some of the basic feelings involved in this kind of illness. If there has been a denial of the very things that make for life, then there must be inevitable frustration which is followed by hostility. This in turn leads to an extremely painful guilt-reaction. One of the main problems in working with the mentally ill person is that the patient does not have the self-respect necessary to face these negative feelings within himself, and hence needs to run away. Perhaps the most devastating thing that can happen to the patient is to have sudden attention drawn to the very feelings he cannot face. This can only serve to aggravate the original injury, and further weaken the fabric of the patient's self-respect. Above all else, there is needed a supportive and accepting relationship which will create for the patient an emotional climate in which he can feel free to look at some of the things from which he has been running away. This is both a basic responsibility and an opportunity.

Loss of Selfhood

We frequently find that our patients lack a feeling of *identity*. On careful investigation we learn that lack of emotional security in the formative relationships of life has resulted in confusion as to who or what they are as persons. Again, each of us has difficulty in achieving identity, or in *maturing* into a unique and sufficient self. It has been said that the mentally ill are like us, "only more so." This is perhaps the key to the understanding of mental illness—it is the exaggeration, the carrying to extremes of feelings, thoughts and behavior common to all mankind.

As the confusion of identity deepens, as reality comes more and more to be denied and evaded, the person becomes increasingly isolated from his fellow men. As early as 1834, Søren Kierkegaard in his *Concept of Dread* saw mental illness or the very disturbed patient whom he called "the demonic," as exhibiting "shut-up-ness unfreely revealed."[5] He emphasized that the things the individual did and said were all attempts at disguise, revealing a basic fear that he would come to be recognized for what he felt himself to be—totally different and *bad* in relationship to others.[6] It is when the *hidden* or "shut-up-ness" can no longer remain so, and threatens to be revealed, that we can say that the individual has been *possessed* by the illness —which is in itself an attempt to deny the knowledge of the *hidden*. It is the very powerlessness to control or avoid the thoughts, impulses and wishes which seem to overwhelm him that arouses such frank terror in the disturbed individual.[7] For the religious worker this has untold meaning.

In the language of Kierkegaard, mental illness can also be seen as a "dread of the good."[8] By the term "good" he meant essentially that which has to do with the capacity to be oneself, to be free and thus able to choose what is needed for real living.[9] He sees mental

---

[5] Søren Kierkegaard, *The Concept of Dread*, trans. Walter Lowrie (Princeton, N.J.: Princeton University Press, 1946), p. 110.

[6] Here the patient wrote: "On totally different you're right. On 'bad' no. 'Wretched' would be better. I grew up acceptable to the other people around me only on a level *other* than what I really was, implying *that* was not acceptable. I lost my identity right there. At an older age I tried to get it back, but it was gone—there was nothing to it. I could not know that it was not gone; it was just no more than born for development—but same difference. I was 15 years old, the fake me. I could hardly go back and catch up with it. And so I grew older and starved all the more, no matter what I pretended to be, other than chased by the police, not real at all. The mental hospital. Easy to have an identity there. You're crazy. So I acted accordingly. Voices—no I did not hear them. I only saw a light and experienced the hand taking mine, which I am still not at all sure was an hallucination. I didn't really get sick until *one night it came into my head that with the dawn of the coming day I would be found out for what I was—even a fake mental patient!* All I remember of what happened was that with the dawn, having been awake terrified all night, I pulled the mattress over on top of me and hid between it and the springs (how I don't know, being tied down to begin with) and tried to scream the attendants away with 'I'm dead and gone! Go away! I'm dead and gone!' "

[7] See Dr. Anton T. Boisen's *Exploration of the Inner World* for a very illuminating discussion.

[8] Kierkegaard, *The Concept of Dread*, p. 109.

[9] Here the patient commented: "Nothing really—just think it could be said better. 'Free' to choose doesn't necessarily mean 'able' to choose you know. That word 'free' has come to mean more lost than found to me, and I know there are others who must think of it that way too in the backs of their

illness also as a dread of God. He points to the experience described in the New Testament when Jesus was confronted by the Gadarene demoniacs. They were quoted as crying: "What have we to do with Thee, thou Holy One of God? Art thou come to torment us?" "Depart from us!" (Matt. 8). This, in rather vivid expression, is the language of people who feel that by virtue of what they are, have been, and would like to do, they are fit only for punishment and ostracism. A tremendous sense of guilt[10] is evident and a consequent feeling of the patient's being different from the rest of mankind, often most poignantly expressed in symbols. We believe it is thus that mentally ill patients come to feel they *ought* to be punished, *ought* to be ostracized and *do* belong in such a place of known stigma as the mental hospital.[11] In such feelings one can readily find the real clue as to why the mentally ill so often feel that they are the forsaken of God.

Herein lies the pastor's most significant opportunity with these deeply troubled people.[12] With all the patient's feeling of guilt and

---

minds. If you mean free in the found sense, that's something else again. But how many will know?"

[10] Here the patient wrote: "You know something? You're all wet. We do not, at that point, feel guilt anymore—distinguish from good or bad even. All we feel is failed somehow, in a way so big that finger-pointing in any direction would be pure foolishness. We fear the 'good' yes! But not because we are 'bad.' Because GOOD is bad. Figure that out. I can't. But I know it's true. I remember the feeling better than I would like to—an aching emptiness about it more than anything else with wild moments here and there out of sudden desperation, and then back to what's-the-use. 'Good' and 'bad' have about as much meaning as the buzz of flies when it's like that. And God? God is just a word that meant something once but it's gone."

[11] Again the patient's reaction: "We don't feel OUGHT to be punished, ostracized and such so much as simply born to be. I can't forget that invisible tail I used to have that swished when I walked and got in my way when I tried to sit down and whichever way I finally charged around after it, it went the other way. I never said anything. They would have just laughed, and it wasn't funny—or waggled their heads wisely, and it was beyond wisdom. Never did I question why—I just dumbly accepted. Not dumb-headed. Dumb-hearted. Like wars must get people after awhile after enough bombs have fallen on them. Some things just ARE—and you *have* to be 'punished' as you put it— and when people start talking *ought-to-be's* you can't help but wonder to yourself how did *they* escape."

[12] Here the patient wrote: "Is this what you mean to say really? I get the unpleasant idea that 'opportunity' means he's going to get something off of us

34   A PASTORAL VIEW OF THE MENTALLY ILL

shame, with the apparent verification (by his hospitalization) of his feelings of self-condemnation and ostracism, the last person he expects to have call on him is a *man of God*.[13] If the minister does call, the patient feels it must be to condemn or to upbraid him. This sets the stage for the kind of religious interview which of necessity must be based on a friendly supportive relationship, best illustrated by a creative listening attitude in which the patient comes to feel reasonably free to share some of the concerns that have made life so painful for him.

---

while we're in this condition unable to fight back—more realistic maybe than you know."

[13] The patient's comment here is most pertinent: "Same feeling as before about this—only partly true, and that part a small part. More of us don't care anymore than feel guilty or ashamed. WE JUST DON'T CARE ANYMORE. Sight of a minister is a shock only because it is so ridiculous at that point."

CHAPTER TWO

The PASTOR'S AUTHORITY

"They were astonished at his teaching, for his word was with authority . . . [They] wondered at the gracious words which proceeded out of his mouth . . . And they were all amazed and said to one another [in response to the healing of a man with a demon] 'What is this word? For with authority and power he commands the unclean spirits, and they come out'" (Luke 4).[1]

What indeed is this word, this power, this authority? Clearly it is to be "good news": release from bondage, the recovery of sight, liberty from oppression—a new life! This is the heart of Jesus' sermon. That it has to do with the person of Jesus appears equally the import of the Gospel. Here in a living, breathing person the word has become flesh—meaning and truth have come alive—and we are no longer in doubt as to the meaning of ultimate reality! What He was with others—Himself: open, responsive, reaching out, genuine, gracious—this is the authority of Jesus. It is no wonder that men reflecting about Him after the event said that God was in Him reconciling the world unto Himself.

As we read the record we find in Jesus One who really came to know what was His own. He knew who He was. He found Himself rooted and grounded in the Being of God. This is why He could say: "I and the Father are one. He that hath seen me hath seen the Father." These are not arrogant words, arrogant as they sound. They are statements of fact!

Jesus had found the ultimate meaning of life in living relationships with others. This could be called "encounter," "a life of

---

[1] Scriptural references are from the *Revised Standard Version* of the Holy Bible, copyright 1946, 1952 by the Division of Christian Education, National Council of Churches.

dialogue," even "a social theory of personality." Perhaps this is what He meant when He avoided *truth* as an abstract and said "I am the way, and the truth and the life." His authority came from knowing what was in man, because He had been with men. As one truly enters into relationship with others, one has entered into the Ground of Being—God Himself.

This, too, is the nature of the minister's authority in pastoral care. It is the authority of being—the authority of function—of being able to stand with courage in the Ground of Being just as we are—naked and unashamed, but to stand! It means to be able to be what we are, yet responsive to and seeking to understand that which another is. As Jesus was concerned, so too is clinical pastoral care concerned with preaching "the acceptable year of the Lord." This is to seek out the lonely, the frightened, the confused and the bewildered. These are the captives of their hidden feelings, blinded to the realities and in need of release. These are the battered—the deeply troubled people all around us.

It is from these people that we can learn the most. In seeking to know them through genuine sharing of ourselves with them, we can come to speak graciously and truthfully and with authority. In this sharing we too will come to know ourselves and that which binds us one to another and to God.

But our sharing must be genuine. It must be honest! We must have some real knowledge of what we are doing, even though such knowledge may be painful. Our deeply troubled people can testify eloquently both to the ambiguities and the dishonesty they have found in their relationships with those who mattered most to them.

The Need to Hate

In this painful search for self-understanding we inevitably come upon perhaps the hardest of all the sayings of Jesus. It is no accident that it is recorded by Luke, a physician. It speaks to the most difficult of all our relationships, family life, in which we either find or lose our identity as persons. Jesus said: "If any one comes to me and does not hate his own father and mother and wife and children and brothers and sisters, yes, and even his own life, he cannot be my disciple. Whoever does not bear *his own cross** and come after me, cannot be my disciple" (Luke 14:26–27).[2]

Dare we conclude from this that only as we can learn to hate so shall we be able to live? To the truth of this many of us can testify from working with deeply troubled people. It is only when the troubled person has learned that he has been held in bondage by ties of unrecognized and hidden feelings in relationship to those who are closest to him—those who indeed gave him his existence—and then comes to be able to separate himself from those who are so important to him, that he can ever really achieve an identity of his own. The painful fact of life is that such separation cannot occur without recognized and consciously experienced feelings of hatred. It is only as we have found the courage to hate that we can really learn to love! It is only when we have painfully been able to achieve our *dignity* as persons, that we can live with others so that what happens to them matters just as much as though it happened to us. This is a central concern in love. And when we are able to love we can be reconciled one to another.

These are indeed shocking words. But unless we can take them seriously how else are we to understand Him who said, "Do not think that I have come to bring peace on earth; I have not come to bring peace, but a sword. For I have come to set a man against his father, and a daughter against her mother, and a daughter-in-law against her mother-in-law; and a man's foes will be those of his own household" (Matt. 10:34–36).

It would seem that only as we are able to bear the anxiety aroused in us by such feelings can we understand the wisdom, the graciousness and the courage which made it possible for Jesus to share them with us. It wasn't easy for those who heard His first sermon that day so long ago. True, they "wondered at the gracious words which proceeded out of his mouth." But before He had finished ". . . all in the synagogue were filled with wrath. And they rose up and put him out of the city, and led him to the brow of the hill on which their city was built, that they might throw him down headlong" (Luke 4:28–29).

---

* Italics are author's.
[2] See also note page 68, Chapter Four.

If I read this experience correctly it is no wonder that they were angry. It is not proper for a son to come home after establishing a reputation abroad and pointedly remind us that others are more receptive to the truth! Especially is this true when those others are outsiders. He must have learned from this painful experience, because Saint John reports that on the eve of His crucifixion he said to His disciples: "I have yet many things to say to you, but you cannot bear them now" (John 16:12).

It is my conviction that unless we understand more clearly and take more seriously the hidden feelings we have toward those who are *closest* to us, we stand in serious jeopardy of not finding our essential dignity as persons. Chaplains, doctors, nurses or members of other helping professions who minister to the deeply troubled can testify painfully to the tragedy of the shut-up-ness which is so much a part of their living. How else can we account for the excessive use of tranquilizers and alcohol, for accidents, drug addiction, infidelity, mental and physical illness, delinquency and the enmity we all harbor? These are the symptoms of desperate people who neither know themselves nor are known by others. They daily live in the fear of being discovered for what they are; and yet timidly but anxiously they reach out for that help which is often promised but is so seldom delivered. This is what we so often find when we seek out the deeply troubled person.

The Need for Understanding

What is needed above all else is someone sensitive to the hidden, often complex, deeper needs of troubled people—someone who is trained to understand these needs. For the troubled person these needs are not easily articulated. In most cases they must be disguised, and, if perceived, are often only dimly sensed as troublesome. But to the clinically trained person, one of the most hopeful aspects of his ministry lies in the fact that he can recognize the very disguises used as signs pointing to the difficulty itself and the means of its resolution.

In an attempt to make clear what I have been trying to say let me cite two illustrations. The first comes from contemporary literature, Brian Moore's deeply sensitive *The Lonely Passion of Judith Hearne*.[3] Let it be clearly understood that what Brian Moore has written is neither satire, nor a criticism of the Roman practice of confession. It is a frank recognition of the lonely tragedies in which we are all bound—and their inevitable and devastating consequences, unless there is understanding intervention.

Judith Hearne, a spinster, having completely failed at establishing a relationship with a man, is making a confession. She has just been shaken to the roots as a result of two episodes where she had drunk to excess. This she has just mentioned—and speaks of her loneliness.

"I'm all alone and I'm afraid because I don't feel well sometimes and a drink seems to help me. I know it's sinful, and I know I should pray more, and . . ."

But she stopped speaking. She had seen his face. A weary face, his cheek resting in the palm of his hand, his eyes shut. He's not listening, her mind cried. *Not listening!*†

He began to speak: "Now, my child, we all have burdens put upon us in this life, crosses we have to bear . . . Now, I want you to say five Our Fathers . . ."

Her penance said, she started a rosary to Our Lady. Perhaps through prayer, hard prayer, she could conquer her fears, her troubles. If what Father Quigley said was true, she had a family. The Holy Family. They would help her.

But as she said the second mystery, she stopped and gazed at the faraway altar. What good, if even God's anointed priest did not understand? He did not listen, he cut me off, nicely, of course, but he cut me off. And the rude way he told me I shouldn't be having my confession heard at this time . . . We all have burdens, he said. As if he didn't want to hear them, don't bother me with your troubles. An ignorant man. God's anointed, with God's guidance, he should have known it was important, perhaps the most important confession of my life. But he didn't see that. And if he didn't see, why didn't You tell him, O Sacred Heart, why didn't You guide him, help him to help me? Why?

---

[3] From *The Lonely Passion of Judith Hearne*, copyright © 1956 by Brian Moore, by permission of Atlantic-Little, Brown and Company (Boston).
† Italics are author's.

After a blinding episode of drunkenness, Judith Hearne makes one last desperate attempt to talk to the priest. When she is not heard she loses her remaining sanity and in desperation tries to find God by attempting to tear open the tabernacle. One of the kneeling housewives, who had witnessed the debacle, asked Father Quigley:

"Why did she do it?"

And he looked down at the bloodstained hands, the bruised face and straggling hair of the woman in his arms. He looked and then he looked at the locked tabernacle.

"God knows," he said.

In this illustration the author exercises his literary prerogative, and makes his point shockingly. In the life situation which I use next, everything is much more subtle—those who would understand must develop the ability to discern that which is only barely hinted. What I shall now quote is a brief English composition written by a deeply troubled university student the night before he committed murder. The essay is entitled: "Is Life a Bore, or Is Man a Bore Within the Realm of Life?"

Today man is living in a diversified life, but because he is held to a constant and routine form of living, he sometimes is unable to touch these diversities and enjoy them. Man seems to feel that because he lives everyday the same, he has become a robot who works like an assembly line, never stopping and never going anywhere, just moving. The world moves so quickly that passing enjoyments lead only to needed wants and anxiety. When one cannot have them, he becomes bored and finally develops unhappiness.

Then again life may not be a bore, but man has made himself boring. He has not wanted to change and has considered everything unexceptional. Instead he sits only to complain about lack of nothing to do. In *Life* magazine there was a picture in an article about the Debutante set, of a well-groomed young man slouched in a chair and wearing a bored look. Here was a fellow who presumedly had the social necessities, money, looks and the fancy women. But he was still looking for more exciting things to do. Another boy would feel that his present enjoyment was wonderful. This shows that anything can become tiresome, or that satisfaction is unattainable because some have to [sic] much and others haven't enough.

Why doesn't the human assembly line stop, let everyone off and let the people do as they please until they become bored with that, and so rejuvenate with new inspirations to become a human tool of production again. Soon the diversities that were looked upon by man as enjoyment will become less exciting and new excitements will become enjoyment.

Life is a pattern which can cause people who live within it to become stereotyped. Because of this man has provided for such circumstances, by being creative, vacationing, and in some occasion attending movies and watching television. Not all people can become a rancher, millionaire, or beatneck [sic]. Each man must aid in the world corporation of human existence by providing for himself and looking after his interest in life. Statistically ten percent of the hundred and seventy million people in the United States are unhappy with their work. This causes boredom and mental confusion. Today man has not found himself in this fast confusing world of ours. To be born in the twentieth century means competition, hard work and enjoyment. The two previous factors are the causes for routine and continuous labor, for which the latter is a reward.

Today man can become more of a bore through his own wants rather than letting life contribute to it. Man has developed a pattern of life which we all live in. Thus man must not let himself down, and become a piece of clay which other forces can mold."

This composition was given to a clinically trained teacher with no indication as to its origin. The question was asked of the teacher: "What does this composition tell about the atmosphere and attitude of the writer?" The teacher replied:

"This is a very confused student. The paper suggests that the student is seriously struggling with something but hasn't caught it. It—what the student is struggling with—seems to me to be a core issue of our contemporary culture, but the student is frightened by it. There are obvious evidences of anxiety and the evasion and denial of anxiety here. He almost seems to be saying, don't take me too seriously; I'll give you a battle but I'm not persuaded of myself. The content is confused—it is as though the student is trying to say something but is afraid to. The student feels naked, ashamed, vulnerable—afraid to be hurt, but has already been hurt quite a bit. It's a sick paper—here is somebody searching and asking for help— even begging for help. *If I received such a paper I wouldn't grade it, I'd ask the student to come in and talk with me. He needs to talk to somebody who has some understanding.*"

The most important point about this illustration is the demonstration that deeply troubled people do give signs of their turmoil and that these signs can be identified by those clinically trained to be sensitive to them. To be able to see the signs is a necessity if tragedy is to be forestalled and help offered. Ministers can be trained to understand these deeply hidden, often complex, emotional needs and an effective ministry can be offered not only to the alleviation of human misery, but even to the saving of human life.

Let us now look carefully into an experience Jesus had with His disciples. When Jesus came down from the Mount of Transfiguration He found His disciples perplexed by their inability to heal a sick boy given to violent seizures. The disciples as well as the father of the boy appealed to Jesus for help. After the boy was helped the disciples asked Jesus why they had been unable to do as He did. His comment was very brief: "This kind cannot be driven out by anything but prayer" (Mark 9:29).

The Need for Training

Could it be that Jesus meant that in order to perceive the nature of some of the deep inner trouble from which we suffer, a great deal more time and painstaking preparation must go into the training of those who would minister in His name? I have no hesitation in saying that I would read at least this meaning into His words. Daily we are becoming more acutely aware of our need for just such careful and diligent preparation of our future pastors. This is why more and more seminaries are requiring some kind of clinical pastoral preparation before men reach ordination.

However, let us examine how little is really being offered in the face of the serious needs. Today a student rarely gets more than three months of full-time clinical experience in his three years of seminary life. Yet many of us are convinced that unless a man has had one year of full-time clinical experience he is not really ready to be a pastor to his people. This is directly in line with the Niebuhr-Williams-Gustafson report in *The Advancement of Theological Education*.[4] Let me quote: "Firsthand experience with persons in trouble is the basic material out of which Christian skill in care of souls must come." The report gives strong encouragement to the development of a fourth and clinical internship year in theological education.

A physician desiring to practice psychiatry must spend five years in clinical experience, *after* one year's internship, and *before* he is allowed to sit for his examinations as a psychiatrist. Surely we in the ministry should give serious attention to spending more time in our clinical preparation! If we do not, we may find true the words of Dr. Erich Fromm. This eminent psychoanalyst maintains that by virtue of his training and personal preparation the psychoanalyst is rapidly taking the place of the clergyman in being a "physician of the soul."[5]

Do not misunderstand me. I do not wish to be interpreted as saying that all future ministers should spend a year in a hospital or prison for their clinical *pastoral* preparation. I have come to feel that such a plan might indeed be dangerous in view of the way many modern clinical training programs have evolved. But this is one of the areas of major confusion in which we are caught today. It is a basic issue with which we who are engaged in clinical pastoral education must continue to struggle seriously. Here is where we are in deep need of expert theological and psychiatric criticism of existing clinical pastoral training programs.

I believe that a seminarian should *begin* his clinical preparation in the more controlled environment of an institution under the competent guidance of a clinically trained chaplain supervisor. Before ordination however, he should spend at least six months in a supervised parish-centered program, working with parishioners. Such training must be under the careful guidance of a clinically trained

[4] H. R. Niebuhr, D. D. Williams and J. M. Gustafson, *The Advancement of Theological Education*. (New York: Harper & Row, Publishers, 1951), pp. 122, 219.

[5] Erich Fromm, *Psychoanalysis and Religion* (New Haven, Conn.: Yale University Press, 1950).

pastor capable of utilizing to the utmost the experiences of the parish.

The need for more and better clinical pastoral preparation of the future pastor is important and demanding. However, at this time in theological education our most acute need is for more competent and adequately trained clinical teachers or supervisors. To this need we must now seriously address ourselves. It may well be that churches will find that a *supervised* ministry of *learning*, even if maintained at the expense of curtailing pastoral services, will achieve a degree of effectiveness which will more than justify the necessary sacrifices.

To become a competent pastoral supervisor requires, in my judgment, two full years of clinical preparation, which should be undertaken only after the candidate has graduated from seminary and satisfactorily completed a period of parish ministry. He would then return for his clinical preparation and his graduate theological studies. This future clinical teacher would work full-time in a hospital setting and in addition pursue studies which would enable him to think seriously and critically about the basic theological concerns related to his clinical work.[6]

Though the clinical training movement has managed to establish some guide-lines in this new venture in theological education, there are still many vast areas that need to be explored and charted. However, some things have become clear. In the field of clinical learning the student can and does come to grips with what is going on between himself and other people. This has not been an easy lesson to learn. Only when we who seek to minister to others have first entered the arena of interpersonal anxiety and allowed ourselves to become exposed to our own as well as to other people's anxieties, can the most meaningful learning take place. How painful and difficult this is becomes a little clearer when we find that anxiety itself restricts and confuses our awareness of what is actually going on between ourselves and others. But the best learning takes place in a relationship where, under supervision, the material for discussion is what two or more people experience with each other; what they

---

[6] See Footnote 2, Appendix for a more detailed description of such a program as it is being worked on at Wesley Theological Seminary and Saint Elizabeths Hospital, Washington, D.C.

do to each other, and how these things are done. It is here that recognition of the negative and denied feelings and experiences of life of which we are all too often ashamed—our doubts, perplexities, distortions and resentments—can often be the means by which new life is possible. One has indeed joined the human race the day he accepts the truth that God is great enough to accept him just as he is. Only then does he become free to grow into that for which we say he was divinely intended. The point of beginning is that then he also is able to accept himself. Perhaps in part this is what Jesus had reference to in His often quoted: "You will know the truth, and the truth will make you free" (John 8:32).

The basis of authority in pastoral care is, therefore, the authority of a new understanding, a new sensitivity and skill in meeting people. Having entered, under expert guidance, the many areas of human distress which are found in the lives of our deeply troubled people, the student minister emerges with a new orientation and competence in his pastoral relations. He comes out better able to share of himself—rooted and grounded in the Being of God. He is now able to listen; to open himself to new experiences; to avoid shutting himself or the other off in the midst of anxious communications; even to obtain new and deeper understanding, concern and ability to reach out to the separated others. This, then, can make his ministry a medium of grace and truth mediating the infinite richness of compassion and care.[7]

---

[7] Such formulations arouse acute anxiety in many who appear to be secure only when the traditional modes for expressing the faith are used. Soon after this formulation of the meaning of the minister's authority first appeared in print (the October 1962 issue of *Pastoral Psychology*, "The Minister's Authority in Pastoral Care") a very emotional outburst came from the Reverend Frederick C. Wood, Jr., in *The Union Seminary Quarterly Review* (January 1963—"Kerygma and Therapy: The Pastor's Dilemma"). He stated ". . . from somewhere must soon be heard the smash of fist upon desk and a loud 'nein' to this kind of foggy thinking concerning the nature and authority of the ministry." Though Mr. Wood's article does touch upon some crucial issues about the pastor's dilemma, issues in which we are all caught and with which we are seriously concerned, it reveals an astonishing naïveté concerning "proclamation" as verbalization, and "proclamation" as witness. Any student with even a rudimentary knowledge of this field has usually indicated that he has been able to clarify this issue before he is permitted to continue his "advanced" studies. In addition, Mr. Wood almost totally fails to understand the

If we have understood correctly what our Lord was saying about one's "foes being those of his own household," parents would do well to assist their children in their periods of rebellion and separation. Then perhaps we may not find so much terror in our aloneness but may say with the confidence of the Psalmist: "When my father and mother forsake me, the Lord will take me up . . . [for] I had utterly perished unless I had believed to see the goodness of the Lord in the land of the living" (Ps. 27:10, 13). To make this possible we need, above all else, the influence of a "healing community"—an atmosphere where we can be accepted for what we are, and just as we are, and thus be freed to become more than we are. Thus we may be able to achieve something of that high dignity for which we believe we were created as sons and daughters of God.

It is in this community that the informed and sensitive pastor should be able to play the distinctive and most needed function of leadership. To him is entrusted the rich wisdom of the Scriptures and the Church. From both he can draw upon experiences which give meaning to our commitment, purpose and communion in the business of living together as human beings. Then perhaps, God willing, it may no longer be necessary to go through the farce of settling for intimacy without relationship and find ourselves cheated by relationships that have no intimacy. *Then* we need no longer remain hidden. We can affirm our unique identity—be the persons we really are. *Then* we will have achieved the courage to see life clearly, to see it steadily, and to see it whole.

---

import of my formulation and makes the mistake of drawing his quotations out of context. Such writing not only fails to achieve even elementary levels of scholarship but is incredible coming from a doctoral candidate in the field of "Psychiatry and Religion" in one of our recognized theological seminaries.

CHAPTER THREE

The PASTOR'S OPPORTUNITY

It has long been recognized that the pastor has a most unique opportunity for service to those who are deeply troubled. Particularly is this so with those whose interpersonal distress is such that it will require above-average time and effort on the pastor's part, and may even lead to hospitalization. In some measure all that will be dealt with in this chapter is related to those who are troubled, but it is intended that these thoughts apply more directly to the pastor's concern about those who are mentally ill.

For purposes of clarification I will attempt to outline six major areas which offer unique opportunities for the pastor and provide for special pastoral contributions.

Prevention

The pastor is about the only recognized professional worker who can, uninvited, enter most homes. Time-honored and accepted, the office of pastoral visitation provides the sensitive and informed pastor with exceptional opportunities to identify emotional difficulties before they have assumed irreversible proportions. It is in this area that the pastor can make a unique and badly needed contribution, perhaps the most effective contribution of all, but it will require of him the kind of clinical pastoral education still only rarely possible in present-day seminary education. More will be said about such training later. Here we need only emphasize that seminaries need all possible encouragement to assist them in setting up such training programs. Recognition of the possibilities for preventive contributions which can be made by sensitive and adequately trained pastors should aid materially in this direction.

Where the pastor understands the value of regular pastoral visits, he can prepare the way for, and enter into, significant pastoral counseling relationships. As the informed pastor goes about his regular visits and comes to be a respected and trusted member of the family, he will be preparing the way for responding to the inevitable questions his people will ask when they face the usual and normal *crises* of living. It is when these *crises*—moments of heightened sensitivity, expectancy and opportunities for spiritual growth—come upon the individual that he needs above all else the listening, concerned and accepting support of somebody who understands not only something of the nature of the experiences but also their spiritual meaning and significance. We need hardly be reminded that at the point of many psychological crises in human living—birth, puberty, mating, illness and death—there have come to be specific religious *offices:* baptism, confirmation, marriage, pastoral visitation, Holy Communion, and funeral services. In every one of these instances the pastor has unique opportunities not only to forestall future emotional turmoil, but actually to use these moments for personal and spiritual growth.

In addition to pastoral visits the minister has another invaluable and unique opportunity for preventive work in his church's program of religious instruction. In this area we have as yet seen only dimly the psychological needs which can be met through an adequate religious ministry of education. I refer here specifically to the inculcation of basic, positive and life-affirming attitudes, and the development of a sense of self-respect and personal worth so urgently needed by the growing person. We know from clinical experience that these characteristics are frequently lacking in the emotionally sick person's makeup. They are the very basics with which the Church is concerned in its program of meaningful religious education.

Here we have time only to draw attention to the almost limitless opportunities available to the pastor for preventive work by reminding ourselves that it is the objective of the Church to mobilize every available resource to help people to change! We have found that the growing individual asks for such help even though his asking may be quite ambivalent or conflictive. From the moment of baptismal instruction to the time of bereavement, pastor and Church alike are called upon for understanding counsel as well as support.

Certainly it is required of us within the Church to think

through again and again our teaching objectives and methods. Only then can we wisely help the individual throughout all his periods of emotional stress. In this task we are greatly indebted to the behavioral sciences for their findings. Much of what has been clinically learned throws considerable light on religious issues and clarifies the avenues by which the Church and its workers can make their own distinctive contributions. That this area of religious concern should be emphasized and is very much needed right now is a matter of major concern to many.

It has been a frequently voiced criticism that clinically trained chaplains are more able clinicians than they are pastors, and are better equipped to diagnose than to offer a helpful religious and pastoral ministry. This observation is all too often correct. In the past, many ministers have been driven to seek clinical training, but because of lack of support from the Church, the training programs to which they have turned, have not given them clinical *pastoral* training. It is becoming increasingly clear that not all clinical training programs can be equated, and that some can even be destructive of genuine religious and pastoral interest. The pastoral emphasis must be retained, for only those who *are* pastors, called to and convinced in that high calling, can genuinely exercise the *pastoral* office. Other counselors may be most helpful to troubled people but only a pastor can meaningfully represent God to them.

Detection

No matter how seriously the pastor goes about his pastoral visitation, and no matter how carefully worked out his church's program may be for religious education, there probably will still be some in his congregation who will show signs of the kind of emotional turmoil which will require care far beyond his ability and the time available to him. These people will need careful referral or perhaps even hospitalization. This is where the pastor can exercise a much needed function of his role.

It is a well-known fact that those with mental illness who gain expert care early in their illness, respond much more dramatically to treatment. The ability to recognize the early signs of illness, and to decide what to do and how to go about it, are important requisites of the pastoral office.

This is an area in which teachers of courses in clinical pastoral training can make some of their most valuable contributions. If a hospital administrator wants just one reason to justify opening his hospital to the clinical training of seminarians and clergymen, it could be to develop this ability in pastors. There are, of course, many other benefits to a hospital in having clinical pastoral training as part of its total program. Unfortunately, however, there are still too many hospital administrators and staff members who have never had much experience with adequate clinical pastoral training programs. Accordingly, they see only the "detecting" functions of the pastor with regard to severe emotional turmoil.

No attempt will be made in this book either to list the signs of severe emotional distress or to outline the detailed steps by which one goes about making certain that mental illness is actually present. My reason for not doing so is that literature in this field is already available and there is no need here to do other than draw the busy pastor's attention to what exists.[1]

What needs to be emphasized is that the pastor's understanding of major emotional distress should be such that he does not get overly anxious and resort to a condemnatory and punitive moralistic attitude. Deeply troubled people need a pastor with more than just the requisite skills to detect the depth and extent of their difficulties. They need one who can communicate meaningfully to them that, come what may, they can never be separated from God's compassion and concern. It is invariably helpful to the troubled parishioner for the pastor to be quite clear as to the limits of his office. Then, when the need arises, the transition to more expert care can be achieved graciously and supportively. It has been found that when the pastor is reasonably secure within himself as a person—when he knows what he believes, who he is, and to what he is really committed—the ways he uses to go about detecting signs of serious emotional illness and the means he uses to help people recognize their need for more expert help are really legion. He is then free to choose those

---

[1] See Bibliography.

which suit the needs of the occasion and the person of the parishioner, as well as his own needs.

Toward Hospitalization

We have learned from experience that where the pastor has a good relationship with his people, knows something about living, and is pastorally competent (here again we are confronted with the invaluable contribution of *clinical* pastoral preparation), he is usually trusted and listened to when hospitalization is indicated. It is often quite possible to be frank and direct about the parishioner's need, and get a cooperative response, if the above-mentioned conditions exist.

When the family doctor or psychiatrist recommends hospitalization, his motivation is sometimes quietly questioned by members of the troubled person's family. This questioning does not generally occur when the pastor recommends hospitalization. He is considered to be impartial and free of vested interests. Nevertheless, the pastor will want to guard himself against any tendency toward self-glorification and status-seeking in the helping role. He will especially need to know the boundary lines of his competence so that referral can and will be made when he can no longer be helpful in the counseling situation. At such a time the pastor will state the facts in a clear, calm and convincing manner so that the troubled person will agreeably decide to seek the help of a more specialized professional.

What is meant by "stating the facts" in a situation like this? Without going into any complicated detail, just this: If, after seeing the pastor a dozen or so times about some specific distress, the parishioner has achieved no significant alteration in either feelings or behavior, it is time for the pastor to think of referring him to somebody better trained and with more time.

How this will be dealt with depends very much on the individual pastor, but at least this framework is clear: The pastor will clearly draw attention to the evidences of his parishioner's distress, pointing out that they have been working together now for a stated period of time, and that the pastor recognizes more help is required than he has either the skill or the time to give. Fortunately, the pastor is in a position to make a competent referral, and he encourages his parishioner to consult the person he recommends.

He could stop right there, but we have learned that a little more uncomplicated directness can often achieve the needed results without any violation of the integrity of the parishioner. The pastor may offer to make an appointment with the specialist when the parishioner is ready to follow up his initial recommendation. Having done this the pastor must then be able to leave his parishioner free to make the final decision for himself.

Of course, there are exceptions to such a procedure. What if the parishioner is much too sick or confused to take the needed steps? What is to be done if he is a potential threat to himself or to others? There is no adequate substitute for the pastor's making clear his understanding and concern to the nearest relative just as he would have done to the parishioner himself as suggested above. The final choice or determination should then be left to the relative.

If there are no relatives, or if the relatives refuse to act, the pastor has no alternative but to use his best judgment. Some way can usually be found for a medical consultation, especially since such troubled people usually have difficulties with sleeping or eating or both! If it develops that there are either strong homicidal or suicidal tendencies, the medical person could institute the necessary legal steps. In any case, the only warning I want to offer is this: The wise pastor will avoid insofar as possible becoming known as a "committing pastor" ("see him about a personal problem and you end up in a psychiatric ward or the state hospital!"). Such a pastor quickly learns that his counseling opportunities are seriously curtailed and his pastoral functions restricted.

In working more closely with members of the other helping professions, clinical pastoral training programs can be of great help to the clergyman. It is always helpful to know the objectives and methods as well as the people in other professions, and to be able to draw more clearly the lines of demarcation between the professions. Pastoral institutes for the training of both clergy and psychiatrists are in a unique position to help the busy pastor see more clearly his own role as contrasted with that of the psychiatrist and to clarify the intricacies of when and how to refer a troubled parishioner most effectively. Above all, such programs help the clergyman gain more confidence in his own pastoral opportunities, for it is while conferring with a psychiatrist under supervision that he gains understanding of the uniqueness of the latter's functions, and so comes to differentiate more clearly his own unique contributions. Here, then, we can manage to overcome one of the complaints increasingly being directed at the pastor by the psychiatrist: that the pastor all too often refers parishioners who really are not in need of such referral at all, but could benefit more from the skilled services of an informed and more competent pastor. This has frequently been found to be the case when pastors have referred parishioners during a bereavement crisis when what was needed was a more trenchant use of the pastoral offices so that those suffering bereavement could work through their grief problems in a meaningful and satisfactory way.

One of the points badly needing clarification as we consider this area called "toward hospitalization" is the contribution the pastor can make toward *avoiding* hospitalization. This needs much careful investigation. With the advent of the so-called "tranquilizing" drugs, and the fact that many individuals who once were automatically hospitalized are now being treated in the community, the pastor needs to be all the more alert to the ways in which he can be of help. What has been said so far should give him some specific clues as to how he can develop and further the skills already at his command.

In this connection it would be well to point out that today there is a growing tendency to avoid hospitalization for emotional illness, if at all possible. We have become increasingly aware of the trauma which may be experienced in the act of hospitalization itself. Linkage with the stigma still strongly associated with mental illness, and the real difficulties a former mental hospital patient has in regaining employment, have contributed to this change in attitude. This emphasizes the need for the pastor to be aware of many sources of help other than hospitalization which should be available to his people. It behooves him to become familiar with and perhaps even take the lead in organizing or showing the need for social agencies, pastoral counseling institutes, church clinics, family and group ther-

apy programs, all of which have made significant contributions to
the alleviation of emotional stress.

During Hospitalization

One of the things most frequently mentioned by mental hospital chaplains is the neglect of the patient by his pastor after the
parishioner (now the patient) has been hospitalized. There are
many reasons for this, not the least among them being (since he too
is human) that the clergyman shares in the community's fear of the
mentally ill. Many ministers who have come to us for clinical pastoral training, after they have come to know us and the hospital,
have felt free to admit such fears. These fears have often been denied by these same pastors when they first arrived at the hospital.

However, one of the main reasons for pastoral neglect of hospitalized parishioners has been the fact that the clergyman simply
didn't know what to expect when he arrived at the hospital. Often
he is afraid that he is unwelcome (which is seldom the case unless
he is one of those blundering know-it-alls who tries to usurp everybody's rights) and he does not know what kind of behavior is helpful or non-helpful once he gets there. This is why hospital chaplains
are constantly being encouraged to develop short clinical pastoral
training courses (clinical externships) for the clergy in their com-
munities. The pastor is thereby enabled to learn the distinctions between his own and the chaplain's contributions. Such courses have
inevitably led to an increase of pastoral visits, which have proved to
be beneficial to both the patient and the hospital.

A contribution perhaps only the community pastor can make
to the hospitalized patient is that by visiting the patient he gives con-
crete evidence of the congregation's concern about the patient—when
the patient expects it least. This is a contribution no chaplain can
make, regardless of his training. The chaplain cannot and should not
try to take the place of the patient's own pastor. A pastoral visit can
gain enormously in meaning when it is followed by additional signs
of the Church's concern as the pastor encourages individuals and
church groups to take an active and volunteer interest in the hospital, its program and the patients.

Community clergymen who do visit their people while they are patients in the hospital are often uneasy about their role when the patient is critical or condemnatory about the hospital or its staff. It is often very helpful for them to learn that one of the most salutary aspects of hospitalization is just the fact that the patient *can* give free vent to his negative, hostile and critical feelings. Indeed, often the illness is inextricably caught up in the prohibitions, actual or fancied, the patient had experienced in the community about these feelings.

Thus the clergyman is not called upon to take sides when these criticisms are voiced. It is enough for the patient to know that the clergyman has sufficient understanding not to be taken in by the negative feelings as being the only feelings the patient has. Such knowledge doesn't really have to be verbalized by the clergyman, though where he does have the requisite understanding and experience with mentally ill people, his articulation of these understandings can be most helpful to the patient in further alleviating the dreadful sense of loneliness experienced in his isolation.

We have already drawn attention to the fact that the mentally ill are *hurt* people; we need now to be reminded that they also have an unusual capacity to hurt others. As a matter of fact, it is their almost unbounded ability to irritate, antagonize and offend that has led many people to believe that "mental illness *is different from* any other illness." In this respect it is different. But it is my contention that to emphasize this is to perpetuate the stigma associated with mental illness. Certainly the mentally ill tend to offend, but if we are not too threatened by their offensive ways, in fact can recognize in them our own more cleverly disguised ways of dealing with difficult people, we can soon come to appreciate the clues to means of healing and reconciliation that are to be found in these painful maneuvers. Above all, it is incumbent upon the pastor to engage in considerable heart-searching so that he may gain more understanding in these areas.

The Pastor and Rehabilitation

In many ways this area is another where pastor and Church together have much to offer the mentally ill patient. This has become more apparent of late since we in the Church have become more sensitive to the basic needs of the mentally ill as a result of the work of hospital chaplains, and the general increase in the public's interest in the mentally ill. In addition, due to the use of drug therapy within the hospitals, many patients who at one time just didn't seem to respond to any treatment have become ready for rehabilitative measures.

It will be possible here to give only brief suggestions for ways in which the church and pastor can work toward more effective rehabilitative measures. These all begin while the patient is full-time in the hospital. They can consist of such ventures as a church group adopting a ward, especially a ward in which there is a member of the congregation. This will require considerable tact and understanding on the part of the visitors, something which should be required in any case. It is just such tact and understanding that the volunteer services of the mental hospital seek to develop in all their volunteers through their training programs. One of the basic factors in determining the effectiveness of a volunteer services program is how well developed and helpful is its training of volunteers *before* they meet patients.

Members of the church either as individuals or as groups should be encouraged to spend some time in the hospital on Sundays. Here they can assist ward personnel in getting patients to church, and by accompanying the patients to church provide convincing evidence of their acceptance of the patient. Indeed, *to worship with* a patient, sitting, standing and kneeling beside him, breaks through the barriers of fear, suspicion, ignorance, misunderstanding, stigma and alienation—all of which are still too often the lot of the mentally ill today.

It would be helpful, too, while the patient still needs continuous hospitalization, if some means could be found whereby discussion groups within the hospital could be joined by regular church-group visitors. Here, as in other activities, considerable understanding and tact is needed, and the fact of regular and constant visits will do much to aid in the patient's rehabilitation. The lack of consistent and trustworthy human relations is often one of the major defects in the patient's history.

The suggestions already given are, in a sense, a prelude to what

is to come. One of the most needed areas which must be explored
in rehabilitation is how a church can arrange for its members to come
into the hospital and work *with* the patient to help him become a
member of the church group *in the community*. Here individual and
group encouragement of church attendance by the patient and his
participation in church-related activities during the week will be of
marked help to the patient taking the first uncertain steps back to
more normal living.

It may well be that such suggestions can assist the churches to
find a new and more meaningful kind of evangelistic endeavor. Certainly the ideas are realistic, badly needed and can be highly produc-
tive in the area of personal satisfactions for the participants. Where
such ventures are attempted the assistance of an adequately trained
and alert hospital chaplain can do a great deal not only for the patients in the hospital as they make their way back into the commu-
nities from which they came, but also for the churches in the com-
munities.

Changing Attitudes Toward Mental Illness

By and large it is still all too true that mental hospitals, their
patients and to a certain extent even those who are on the staff are
all stigmatized and neglected by the total community. The evidences
of this are too readily apparent: inadequate budgets, poorly trained
staff, obsolete buildings and equipment, public apathy and neglect.
In the case of the hospital chaplain, he is still often referred to as
"having left the ministry." Things are changing, it is true, as people
become more aware of mental illness as the major national health
problem. There is still however a very long way to go. In effecting
constructive and lasting change, the church can and must contribute
a very great deal.

In addition to the many suggestions already made, let me venture to add one other.

By no means do all hospitals have full-time chaplains, and
where they do, comparatively few of these chaplains have received
adequate clinical pastoral training. It is by no means an accepted
fact that all hospitals can afford or see the necessity for a full-time

chaplain, clinically trained or not, in spite of the fact that this is one of the standards of the American Psychiatric Association. Here churches have a real opportunity, not only by inquiring about the availability of such chaplain programs but by financially initiating and supporting them where necessary. In this way they can demonstrate that they have a useful contribution to make to the hospital's program. There have been instances where this was done. Such chaplaincies soon became an accepted and integral part of the hospital's financial and treatment program. It soon becomes clear to the alert hospital administrator that no program is fully effective until it meets intelligently the basic needs of its patients. Clinically informed and sensitive pastoral and worship ministries for hospitalized patients have already shown themselves to be a most useful resource not only to the therapeutic program but in changing the public's attitudes toward the hospital, its patients and staff alike. A chaplain trained for his special ministry can become the kind of intermediary between hospital and community that both very greatly need and can use. The scope of such usefulness has by no means been even dimly appreciated.

Under the leadership of a well-trained chaplain, volunteer services can be promoted, the clinical pastoral training of both seminarians and clergymen guaranteed, and the hospital can avail itself of a most effective voice in interpreting its problems and needs to the community. In addition, since the chaplain represents the community as much as the hospital, he can be a means of further stirring up the public conscience to take more active interest in the hospital, its program and problems. Not the least important result might be the more effective integration of treatment, training and research methods and goals, so that these achieve a far greater unity than has as yet been possible in even our best mental hospitals.

In concluding this chapter let me again emphasize that we are only at the beginning of an understanding of the many and varied ways available to pastor and Church for making a significant and abiding contribution to those who are mentally ill. Where these ways are explored and attempts made to effect the suggestions offered, another major step will have been taken to give signal assistance to the most deeply troubled people of our time.

CHAPTER FOUR

SPEAKING
From The WILDERNESS
Of The LOST

The Basic Contribution of Religion to the Deeply Troubled

My own experience with clinical pastoral training was a major turning point in my life. As a result of that training I am increasingly more confident that what we in the Church have to offer—our faith and practice—not only has relevance for all time, but is desperately needed in our time. Above all, I think I know not only *why* but *how* this was possible. If I had but a sentence with which to express it, I would put it this way: When one dares to trust the Gospel to the extent that one descends into the hell which life often is, one cannot escape finding his way to God Himself.

When I was asked to give the Convocation address at the 96th Annual Convocation of St. John's College in Winnipeg, Manitoba, I turned to one of the patients at the hospital for suggestions as to what I might say. This deeply sensitive and gifted young woman had spent almost 15 years of her life in mental hospitals. She has helped me in many ways to *share* what is most important in living together as persons. From her I have gained clearer perspectives for my ministry and teaching, and above all, the courage to be myself.

I shared with her my concern that the occasion be used to say something relevant—something helpful in the business of living. I couldn't think of anything more meaningful than to try in such a presentation to share the heart of what I had learned in my years in the mental hospital. (Our work together at this point was aimed specifically at helping her to return to the community, which she left in 1956 when she came to Saint Elizabeths Hospital.) I asked her: "What is it about people that has made it, and still makes it, hard for you to be a person? As we have talked about the early years of your life, if I have heard you accurately, the strange behavior which was your life seemed to be largely the result of your trying to be true to yourself and still be what was expected of you by those who were important in your living. Let me now ask you, now that you are ready, or getting ready, to go out into the world and to join the human race, what are the concerns which trouble you? I think you know why I'm asking the question—and in this I know we agree—it is to encourage those who can do it to achieve their real identities. Put in another way, it is to help others to take upon themselves the anxieties of living and being real persons. Perhaps we have a special interpretation as to the meaning of being a real person, but here again we agree: to us it means 'being able to allow a little of the loneliness which is me to meet the loneliness which is you.' "

She was quite hesitant—but after only a few hours came back to my office, glowing, and said: "I couldn't do it when you asked—it seemed impossible and I resented your asking—but I couldn't leave it alone either, because it wouldn't leave *me* alone. Suddenly what you had said reached a spot in me and clicked, like a key in a lock, making possible the outpouring of something I have been needing to say for a long time that wouldn't come free before." This is what she had written:

THE VOICE OF ONE WHO IS LOST

Hidden within each of us is something very uniquely ours and precious to God—our real self. For those of us who are resilient and willing to be molded—no especial problem. But for those of us who to various degrees recognize our individuality for the sacred thing that it is, woe unto us at the hands of our parents, teachers, and society, not to mention the woe, in our desperation, that we cause them. There are only about three directions we can go in the name of self-preservation: to prison, to a mental hospital, and as a last resort, self murder. Yes, most of us would rather seal it away safely in death than have it taken from us, for that death is worse.

Fortunate is the child who, amidst the many do's and don'ts and rules and regulations imposed upon him in all directions, retains the feeling of being loved for himself by someone. I suspect rare is that child, too. Love is a priceless thing, and easily misused as a reward for obedience and good behavior. If you do not obey the Ten Commandments and do as mother says, God will not love you—and mother will not love you either. The only thing is—that kind of love is as superficial as the good behavior probably was.

How many times I dutifully divided candy bars with my playmates, keeping the smallest piece for myself, while within my wretched little soul a voice cried out, "No! It's as much of a sin as if you'd kept it all yourself! You don't mean it!" Sometimes I had a feeling dangerously close to hoping they'd get sick on it too. But the love I thus earned I hungrily accepted, my need for it greater than my unworthiness. How sad that love was, for deep inside I did not feel loved or even wanted—for myself—and the need to be myself began to wax stronger than the need to be loved. If the self in me should die, what good love then? I wandered alone about the neighborhood much, strangely comforted by the trees and flowers and sky in my ponderings, and practiced endless hours on the piano, oblivious of time.

Slowly and steadily grew a hatred in me that I could not acknowledge, and I began to pray each night a prayer from so far in the depths of me that I did not understand it myself, though I fervently meant every word of it. "Oh God, please never leave me— no matter what happens—no matter what I do. Please—even if I *tell* you to go, don't do it. Remember back to this—and how much I need you—and don't listen to me." Some fifteen years later, that prayer utterly forgotten, and terribly failed by the Church, I was to dare God to come down in my size and try to tell me what to do—I'd beat Him all over the place. I gave up my religion a moment later when it dawned on me what I had dare feel toward Him.

I was an old pro by then to the mental hospital situation, having first required confinement in 1947 at the age of fifteen. Now, with the old feelings of despair, futility, and inability to go on once more upon me, I faced the prospect of another confinement as one facing death. Indeed, I had been told when they sent me home the previous time that the next time they would keep me for life. Pretty grim, the prospect of just custodial care—while I went ahead and died inside, or went out of my mind fighting it. A cry for help welled up in the soul of me, only to die on my lips. What help? There was no help. Not even God.

Some weeks later the fire chief could not believe me when I told him I did not know why I had set the fires. "Well, what did you feel like?" he persisted. I had not felt anything, I told him. Just empty. They put me in jail, then sent me back to the mental hospital, then back to jail—and finally I was let out on bail until arrangements could be made to send me to Saint Elizabeths. Deep inside a part of me would not be consoled, as real to me as my worldly side, and I often retired to my room and cried uncontrollably. One day Daddy came in and tried to talk, but somehow there was nothing left to say and I could only look at him. "You make it very hard to be a father," he told me, strangely hurt. I could not say anything to that either—not without hurting him worse. He left then, defeated in some way. For a little while longer I cried, then stopped. It didn't matter anymore. I hated myself now too.

When I came to Saint Elizabeths in 1956 enough interest was taken in me to make me really try for awhile. But I couldn't keep up my own end of it, and fast lost support. "You must help *yourself*," they said—but there was no help in me. After some two years of therapy I saw that my therapist could not save me either, and damned beyond redemption, all belief in myself gone, I finally lost contact. This was the death that I had feared worse than death. Mercifully, I did not know.

Months later I awoke one morning and found myself back again. I knew it could be nothing I had done, and I could pretty well be sure that it was nothing anyone else had done either, because it had been bigger than both of us. I remembered how it had been before everything went black, and shuddered. No one could have done this but God! But that would mean that I had been forgiven things that *couldn't* be forgiven. And then I remembered the prayer of my childhood, and overcome, could only whisper through the bars in awe and disbelief: "You remembered!" *I* was more important than my sins.

When you *know* that God is for you, no matter how discouraging the situation—you are lifted above it. And though I was now obviously sick as I could be, I was happy. It was out. It wasn't locked inside of me anymore. I delightedly ran around the ward with a fly swatter for a rod and claimed I was Moses.

Strangely enough, as I improved my faith weakened. Many old questions raised themselves again. Wavering, I accepted a typing position in the Chapel, and walked into something had I been able to find 15 years earlier would have spared me much anguish: a group of people who care about *me* more than my behavior—who hear me and see me for what I am, and understand—who accept me for myself *on a level with themselves!* It has taken me a long time to believe it, because it has taken me a long time to accept myself, let alone find myself in the first place—for I was hopelessly buried under years of denial. Many times I would have given up, but they would not let me. They believed in me. And though I did not believe in myself, I believed in one of them, so I kept trying. It has been like coming into sunlight from the depths of the earth. It is very wonderful—and frightening. But I'm still trying.

And now I see something I did not see before—that I am needed by other people for myself as much as I needed this for my own sake. That what I was before was as inadequate for them as it was for me. It is not just my problem—it is one that we all share in common. No wonder it took so long to find help. They could not help me for their own need of it.

If God should ever come to me and ask me, as He did Solomon, what gift I most desire in all the world, I think I would tell Him "understanding." For I see so many in desperate need of it, and if I could only give it to them maybe I could give them back to themselves as I have been given back to myself. No one else seems to be noticing them. Others need to be saved from themselves, so busy trying to turn themselves into bricks like everybody else that they do not see they are diamonds the way they are. I have even seen chaplains struggling away from themselves, instead of *with* themselves, to something supposedly better—more acceptable—and my response varies from wanting to shake them until their teeth rattle to a need to take them by the arms (so they can't get away) and say: "I think I like you but I don't know—you're all hidden away where I can't reach you and I bet you can't either, which is a dirty trick on both of us you'll see one day. You know something? Most of what you guys say and do doesn't mean a blasted thing to us. We see it for the empty ritual of one sort or another that it is. Why do you keep what we need the most from us?—yourself! Don't you know that if you don't give us something of yourself as a person you can't mean anything to us as a chaplain? Oh glory to skip the How-are-you-Fines sometime and hear you say *hell* from the heart!"

No—God alone is not enough. We need each other too. And though one would never know it, to look at us, I would guess that's why He gave us each other.

Sharing Our Deepest Selves

Implicit in this deeply moving statement is the concern that whoever we are, wherever we are, no matter with whom we are, we be honest with ourselves and willing to share what we are—good and bad—with each other. This is no new insight—this is the priesthood of all believers! This is the willingness to take upon ourselves the burden of the cross, the burden of being human. This is an invitation to join the human race—not to avoid it—for to avoid it is to become "caricatures of what we might have been."[1]

If I understand what has just been said this is vivid testimony to the mentally ill patient's struggle to attain some sense of dignity, integrity and identity. As has already been indicated this makes mental illness a religious problem indeed, because it cannot be understood apart from that which gives meaning to our living: our values, our sense of destiny, our commitments, communion and convictions.

It would appear, then, from what has been said, that we who minister to the mentally ill are in the enviable position of being able to learn and to teach much that is badly needed in our time. What of the brokenness in human families which is so large a part of the histories of our mentally ill? It does not matter whether this brokenness is expressed as incompatibility, alcoholism, drug addiction, chronic mental illness, suicide, infidelity or promiscuity, or whether it is a *hidden* brokenness—the outwardly *model* family situations—it appears frequently in our patients' histories. It is a sign of a profound sense of estrangement from others *with* clues as to how these things come about and how they can be helped. This is why our mentally ill are often our profoundest teachers—and as we give them their due rights as teachers we help them strengthen their terribly weakened self-respect.

The Pastor's Contribution

I consider the pastor's contribution to be threefold in nature. First, we have a distinctive faith and practice to share. In the second place, we have always held important the necessity for careful and

---

[1] Another of Dr. Harry Stack Sullivan's descriptive phrases about people who had only *unhappily* managed the maturing process.

continued self-scrutiny of life's experience with a view toward effecting a greater wholeness in living. Finally, we have held all this
to be "under God" in such a way that we can recognize our depend-
encies for what they are—that is, self-fulfilling. We hold that what
we believe, what we have been and are, can be affirmed un-
ashamedly. We believe that our dependency will not force us to
descend into self-denigration or self-abasement, which is all too often
the rule in the practice of religion.

Religion is not just another function among other functions. It
is a dimension, a way of relating to all other functions. It deals with
man's basic attitudes toward himself, his fellow man, his universe
and his God. When such attitudes are positive and life-affirming
they can lead to helpful and healthy relationships with others.
Though obviously concerned with "faith and morals," such a view
of religion *does not* consider itself simply as a code of conduct. View-
ing religion chiefly as a code of conduct results in the frequently
voiced criticism, and justly so, that much of what goes on in the
name of religion is damaging to the human being.

Our patients are often without any sense of meaning or purpose
in life. They cannot relate the meaning and purpose of life to daily
conduct in human relationships. They often do not even know
what is helpful or unhelpful. It is here that the cardinal concerns
of religion come to the fore. It is at this point we are reminded *again*
that they need above all the sensitive and clinically informed guidance of one who has intimate knowledge of the meanings of commitment, communion and purpose in this business of living together
as persons. Here the understanding minister can do much through
his pastoral calling—his preaching and prayers, his choice of scripture (and the way he reads it) and hymns, his leadership of religious
group discussions—to offer the deeply troubled person a new hope
for life.

Faith and Practice

Faith and practice mean a number of things. In the matter of
faith I suggest not only the repository of what is held as "the truth"
but a trust engendered in a person as a result of the warm, accepting

understanding of those with whom he has been brought up in the household of faith. Hence what is being offered is in no way dogmatically imposed. Through dogmatic imposition truth itself becomes vitiated, for what is forced upon a person can rarely be helpfully accepted and incorporated. True faith—and the practices based on it—must be freely offered and freely shared to have real meaning and value.

None of us lives without some kind of faith. But is our faith explicit or implicit, helpful or unhelpful? We all live by some meaning in our inner workings, even though that meaning be an unacknowledged and much dreaded meaninglessness. This is even more true of our patients who have had such severe struggles with the world from which they have come.

Here again, religion is in a position to make a much needed offering. Standing as it does with the sanctions of the ages in tried and tested beliefs and practices, it offers many reasonably clear guidelines as to that which is helpful and non-helpful in our living. The most important guidelines deal with the questions of ultimate reality—what is *really* meaningful in living, what can be trusted, and what will endure? We need to be reminded that *real* truth, as it deals with persons, is not a vague abstraction but a living quality in our relatedness. Also, our religion teaches that if we want to be clear as to the nature of this living quality—this relatedness—we can look to a particular Person and the way He was with others. Here, as religionists, we make and offer a basic faith assumption: that as Jesus was with others, so God is with us.

It may be of some help to us to remember Jesus' own answer to the vexing question, "What is truth?" As He put it: "I am the way, and the truth and the life." Here we find truth described as a very personal, living, dynamic reality, translated into deeply meaningful interpersonal terms. He even went so far as to say, "He who has seen me has seen the Father . . . I and the Father are one." When His listeners seemed to have trouble in understanding Him, He suggested a very pragmatic test: "Believe me that I am in the Father and the Father in me; or else believe me for the sake of the works themselves" (John 14:11). That is, "believe me because of what you have seen and heard when you were with me."

This is the essence of what the sensitive pastor has to share with his deeply troubled parishioner. To enter into this area, however, is to tread on very personal and holy ground. This is largely the reason we have such difficulty in sharing with members of other professions. But we of the clergy, too, have had much pain in the way this heritage came to us from our parents and significant others; we, too, have had many conflicting feelings about the very truths and practices toward which we aspire. And many of us take a long, long time before we make our peace with these needs.

Self-scrutiny

The second major area of our contribution, the encouragement of a healthy and continuing scrutiny of one's own life, has been no easier. This too has had a very chequered history in its practice. It makes more vivid our anxieties when we do draw closely to each other. It warns us about the pain in tender feelings.

What I am referring to here has often gone on under that misunderstood term of "fellowship." This is referred to in the early pages of the New Testament as an experience of "being together for a considerable period of time." In true fellowship one comes to feel free to share with others some of the certainties and uncertainties of living, some of the real *negativities* that make up our lives— and from which we can gain the most when shared with an openly acknowledged faith in God and His meaning and purpose for us. In other words, "when we dare to be ourselves, naked and unashamed, before God." It takes time, but it can in some measure be achieved, although the Garden of Eden, the state of innocence, has to be left to win such life.

When this emphasis is communicated much liberation comes to the "shut in" and isolated person who is our mentally ill patient. To discover that the Scriptures and sound doctrine are not against many of the feelings his parents and peers led him to believe were *bad,* and that sin is not the petty activities with which many religionists have come to associate it, can be the beginning of a new life for the patient.

Again, for instance, it is most salutary to learn that in the Old Testament we have an understanding of how to resolve the painful break that we must all make with our parents! It says specifically

in Psalm 27:10—"When my father and mother have forsake me . . .",
implying that this separation is expected so that the individual may
come to find a life and integrity of his own. It is then, and this is
found in the same Psalm, that the individual finds "the Lord will
take me up." But poignantly, the Psalmist also adds: "I should utterly
have fainted, but that I believe verily to see the goodness of the Lord
in the land of the living!" (*The Book of Common Prayer*).

It *is* necessary, in the pilgrimage of life, to rebel and to leave
parents, and it is the responsibility of parents to make this possible.
But one cannot become a prodigal to the extent that he cuts himself
off completely from his kind, and *live!* We can never get beyond our
need for concerned others or the healing community—because healing, or wholeness, as we have come to understand it, comes about
with others or *in community*. There is no healing in isolation, only
the alleviation or alteration of the symptoms of our loneliness.

It is here again that I must pay tribute to what many deeply
troubled people in mental hospitals have taught me over the years
about the wisdom of scriptural and theological teaching. The one
illustration their experiences keep forcing me back to is Our Lord's
hard saying, "If any one comes to me and does not hate his own
father and mother and wife and children and brothers and sisters,
yes, and even his own life, he cannot be my disciple."[2] This means
to me that we can never really learn to love unless we first learn to
hate—and find that love is greater than hate. It has also led me, at
least in part, to see in the central act of the Christian religion, the
Holy Communion Service, a symbolic acting out in "the breaking
of bread and shedding of blood" of man's urge to destroy what is

---

[2] Luke 14:26–27. This reference bothers many, as indeed it should.
Biblical interpreters have tried desperately to reassure *themselves* that Jesus
did not really mean or even say "hate." I cannot escape the conclusion that he
did mean just this! Clinically I have seen it happen. What really is hated of
course is the person who, caught up in his own negative ambiguities, *evades*
them by trying to live his whole life through others, rather than grappling with
the painful implications of his own living. Interestingly enough, after I came
to formulate this understanding for myself (see Chapter Two, "The Pastor's
Authority") I ran across Dr. Paul Tournier's *Escape From Loneliness* (published by Westminster Press, 1962) where he states on page 155, "He who
cannot hate intensely cannot love deeply." Perhaps this too is clinical insight
into the nature and meaning of original sin.

most needed and meaningful to him. Here we have a real dilemma, for on the one hand we assume that the basic drive of the personality is toward health, yet we cannot evade the hard facts of man's ancient struggle with negative and contradictory impulses and feelings. The reconciliation of these opposites has not yet been achieved. Perhaps as we delve more deeply into the psychological meaning of "original sin" this may become clearer to us.

If the need to enter into an act of rejection and hate is denied, the individual is never able to separate himself and master his primitive drives, his incestuous leanings, his hateful and destructive tendencies—and to become a person in his own right. When the person achieves this, then it is possible for him to love another as though the other mattered to him as much as himself. For then we will have dared to be ourselves before God and to stand in the Freedom of our creation as unique persons. Then we shall have achieved our essential dignity and integrity as persons.

Recognizing Dependencies as Self-fulfilling

I said earlier that all that was believed and experienced in the minister's offering was done so "under God." The minister recognizes and acknowledges a power beyond himself greater than himself to which he submits joyfully. He does so because he has found the courage to accept himself even though he knows he is unacceptable. He does so because in some measure he has come to terms with the demands of authority and is now able to accept the certainty of some of the things wherein he has been instructed, in spite of the ambiguities surrounding the ways in which they were given and received. He does so because he recognizes in his Ground of Being One who accepts him just as he is: doubtful, confused, bewildered, resentful, hateful and yet striving, hoping, wanting to believe, succeeding and loving—a mortal, lonely human being destined for he knows not what. In short, he believes in and can affirm that God *is!* Then he is in a position to make some progress with what Paul Tillich so eloquently describes[3]—the courage to deal meaningfully with the anxieties of guilt, meaninglessness, and death.

---

[3] *The Courage to Be* (New Haven: Yale University Press, 1952).

It should be stressed that in any work with the mentally ill, what a minister is in himself matters far more than what he does. Only when he has dared to allow himself to experience something of the suffering and joys of his own living, when he has come to terms with his own experiences, is he in a position to appreciate similar feelings in others. As in any work with people, the attitude of the pastor determines the effectiveness of his ministry. If the pastor has a keen awareness of what we have come to regard as *the interpersonal hurt* of his patient; knows the desperate and yet fatal need of the patient to evade further pain, no matter by what means, and often by striking out and hurting loved ones; feels something of the almost overwhelming and intolerable anxiety the patient experiences; is not too shaken by the terror evoked through what Kierkegaard expressed as "shut-up-ness unfreely revealed"; and can accept the consequent intense feelings of guilt and shame which isolate the patient from himself, from others and from God, then his ministry has within it the necessary elements for a supportive and creative experience for the patient.

Fundamentally, in his approach to the patient, the minister seeks to understand what the patient has experienced in his living which has made it necessary for him to become mentally ill. He does his best when he offers the patient the greatest gift he has—the gift of himself, rooted and grounded in the Being of God. His own friendly interest, his own reaching out with concern, his own desire to be helpful through a trained and understanding use of his unique religious resources—these are the things the patient needs. Being exposed to this attitude in the minister, the troubled person comes to feel encouraged to reach out of the loneliness of his isolation for the help which is available. It is this attitude which is basic in any meaningful pastoral ministry. It is through this that the minister makes his most distinctive contribution to the hospital's treatment program for the patient. It is in just this way that the minister is able to demonstrate that he has learned something of the language of those who are in the wilderness of the lost, and can speak relevantly to them and for them about their concerns.

CHAPTER FIVE

ANXIETY
And SOME Of ITS
PASTORAL IMPLICATIONS

To understand the ministry to deeply troubled people as much as we can we would do well to look carefully at a fundamental concept in interpersonal relations, the meaning of anxiety. Anxiety is a phenomenon in our living together, which when understood as described by Dr. Harry Stack Sullivan, gives fruitful new insights into the meaning of religious and Scriptural teachings. It will be profitable to explore the significance of a problem which is basic but still altogether too little understood among us. As we come to see more clearly the implications of this aspect of our interrelatedness we discover many useful clues as to the reasons for so much disharmony in the human family. Though anxiety cannot be equated with sin, as we pursue its meaning we soon come to be profoundly aware of it as a "precondition to sin."[1]

Viewed in these terms the whole concept opens up many new areas for further exploration, and suddenly gives new hope for a deeper understanding of man's "sinful" nature. Such understanding would add a most welcome strength to the minister's pastoral resources as he seeks to help his people find more meaning and satisfaction in their daily living.

What Is Anxiety?

Anxiety is a phenomenon that everyone experiences. It is peculiarly human—it is the price we pay for being human. Yet it is a far more complex phenomenon than our familiarity with it would

---

[1] Reinhold Niebuhr, *The Nature and Destiny of Man* (New York: Charles Scribner's Sons, 1941), p. 182. For a most helpful, brief review of

have us think. It is an important aspect of mental illness, as it is of all human life. It is in mental illness that we see the exaggeration, the intolerable increase of anxiety, and non-useful ways of attempting to deal with it. If we would understand its meaning for others, we must struggle toward some kind of resolution about the meaning and experience of anxiety in ourselves.

Obviously we need to make some kind of basic clinical distinction between anxiety and fear. Broadly speaking, fear is the response to an external stimulus, while anxiety arises in response to an internal stimulus—internalized fear. Anxiety is triggered very often by external stimuli, and we may often be both fearful and anxious. In anxiety however, there is aroused an internal response not only to the immediate threat in the environment, but to previous "fears" that have remained unresolved and that persist in the area outside of immediate awareness. There is no clear and adequate explanation of all this as yet, but both fear and anxiety arise from conditions which are or have been a threat to the life or integrity of the organism.

Dr. Harry Stack Sullivan used to say that anxiety was one experience known to the human being that he would not willingly undergo a second time if he could possibly avoid it, but he was constantly undergoing it because he cannot possibly avoid it. The human will not always avoid fear. He may indeed consciously and willingly put himself into a position in which he may experience fear, but he will never consciously and intentionally get himself into a situation involving anxiety if he can possibly avoid it—anxiety is too painful an experience!

Sullivan spoke of anxiety as "that which one experiences when one's self-esteem is threatened." In his lectures he would point out that one of the ways in which the individual responds to his anxiety—or perhaps, more correctly, to the threat which makes him anxious—is to "become confused and restricted in his awareness of what is going on in his interpersonal relations." When that threat is present—and it is quite frequently outside of clear awareness—the

---

philosophical, biological, cultural and psychological descriptions of anxiety see Rollo May's *The Meaning of Anxiety*, (New York: The Ronald Press Co., 1950).

personality sets in operation certain learned devices, processes, mechanisms—"dynamisms"—by which the person confuses and restricts awareness of what is going on.

The best illustration of this is anger, which we all know so well. It is so magnificent a means for neutralizing anxiety, that Sullivan called it "the curse of interpersonal relations." It is a curse precisely because it works so well. When a person grows angry, he does not recollect very clearly what went on to provoke the anger. When anger arises, it is because anxiety has begun to manifest itself, and the personality is employing anger to confuse and restrict his awareness of what it was that made him so anxious and acutely uncomfortable. In our work with deeply troubled people, whose very "troubledness" is an evidence of their anxiety, it is extremely important that we recognize this.

The ways in which people attempt to handle anxiety are many and varied: each one habitually responds in certain preferred ways, according to his own personality needs. Some use anger and irritation; others may use withdrawal from those around them. Some cannot eat when anxious; others eat more than usual because eating has come to have some meaning of security. Some translate their anxiety into physical illness—the psychosomatic illnesses; some turn it outward toward others in the form of aggressive acts or even frank and open hostility. Some use various combinations of these or other ways of trying to carry on the business of living.

Anxiety and Guilt

There is also a relation between anxiety and guilt, between anxiety and the consciousness of sin. The *feeling* of guilt as differentiated from the *knowledge* of guilt closely resembles the feeling of anxiety—or perhaps we should say is a feeling in which anxiety is a component. The individual's knowledge of having done something which he has been led to consider "wrong," the conviction of having "sinned," is a threat to self-esteem, and anxiety is aroused. Unconscious guilt—a feeling of being unworthy—may result when the individual has done or thought something contrary to his beliefs as to what he *should* have done or thought. He may successfully repress the memory of these thoughts; he may forget them so completely that he cannot recall them even with effort, but the blow to his self-esteem cannot be so successfully dealt with. It is no longer a case of having *done* or *thought* something unworthy, it is a sense of *being* unworthy. So people who have guilt feelings have persistent anxiety. Often this takes the form of what is called "free-floating" anxiety. Since the original cause is forgotten, these people tend to react overly to any situation which produces anxiety, and to attach to this situation the entire load of all the anxiety within them.

Insecurity, anxiety, guilt—these are all intermingled and painful. Those who labor under an excessive burden of these crippling emotions are desperately in need of reconciliation. They need the security of the knowledge of the Love of God for them *as they are* and in spite of what they are, to help them deal with their fears and anxieties.

This knowledge, if it is to combat successfully the powerful emotional forces it would oppose, must be something which has real meaning for them. It is not enough to simply verbalize the Love of God—we must show it to them and experience it with them through the giving of ourselves in Christian love. This then is what we understand by that great Biblical truth that "The Word became flesh and dwelt among us" (John 1:14).

Jesus' Dealings with Anxious People

We may well turn to an actual experience in the life of Jesus. Following the Mount of Transfiguration experience, our Lord began, presumably for the first time, to talk about going to Jerusalem. We are told that He said to His disciples, "The Son of man will be delivered into the hands of men, and they will kill him; and when he is killed, after three days he will rise" (Mark 9:31). But the disciples did not understand what He meant, "and they were afraid to ask him" (Mark 9:32). This latter is a classic example of how anxiety works.

Afraid to ask Jesus! Jesus was their friend! They had been with Him for three years. They must have known of His willingness to help them with any lack of understanding. However, the clue here seems to be contained in the words "they were afraid to ask him." It seems clear that they had caught the implication of His teaching—and were threatened by it—and so could not for the time being explore it with Him.

Such is the nature of anxiety! When we hear threatening news, when we see or are subject to things which reflect upon our self-esteem or endanger our lives, we come to doubt or even to turn from those who are close to us. Things which are most plain to us at other times we just cannot grasp during moments of anxiety. We tend to run away. In this way the disciples tried to put the cross from them. We are told that Peter in his anxiety even rebuked Jesus for talking about it, and later, when his anxiety was intense, he lied and swore and even denied knowing Jesus! Anxiety does indeed paralyze the very functions that make us human.

Undoubtedly at this moment the disciples were already anxious and this unacceptable saying of Jesus increased their anxiety. We may recall that before Jesus made His announcement about going to Jerusalem, He had healed a sick boy with whom the disciples had had no success. It is quite likely that they were more than a little insecure as a result of this failure. Then followed this painful saying, which meant, if it were true, that they would lose their friend who would be crucified. It meant also that they would lose their vocation! If their ministry with Jesus should come to an end they would have to go back to their homes and their friends to face the derision and questioning of those who had probably already looked askance at their identification with the humble carpenter of Nazareth. But even more, if He were to be killed, might not the same thing happen to them?

Here we have more than enough in any life situation to make people anxious. Their confidence in themselves had been shaken by their failure to heal the sick boy; their self-esteem was definitely threatened at the prospect of their having to return home following the failure of their mission; and they stood in imminent danger of death. It was almost inevitable that they should be afraid to ask Him what He meant.

The Disciples' Reactions

How, then, did they deal with their anxiety? What action did they take following Jesus' dramatic announcement? Three things seem to have happened. Here we see some common methods people use in trying to get away from anxious feelings.

First, they began to discuss among themselves who was to be the greatest. We might describe this in another way by saying that they began to *compete with one another* for the "first place" in the new kingdom. Of course they knew intellectually that there were to be no first and second places in the kingdom which Jesus proclaimed. They must have known also that to be "chief," one had to be least of all. But their questions came from no intellectual doubt—just as we find so frequently in the hospital that questionings about a patient's illness and the nature of God do not arise from intellectual doubts. When one's inner security has been jeopardized, it seems almost necessary that one try to make more secure one's place in the outer world. This is very human. Another thing too would come out here as it actually did in their experience—they would get the attention of their leader, who would find it necessary again to explain to them the things concerning the kingdom.

Apparently there followed another method by which they sought to take care of their anxiety. It is also reported that they came to Jesus and said, "teacher, we saw a man casting out demons in your name, and we forbade him, because he was not following us" (Mark 9:38). Do we see here an attitude of superiority? When we are made uncertain it is rather easy and comforting to remind ourselves of the group to which we belong or of the status we enjoy. On this basis we make a desperate attempt to deny the inner painful gnawing of our fears. All this too is very human and inescapable.

We are told finally that in their journey they came to a certain city of Samaria where they were inhospitably received. They returned to Jesus quite angry and recommended that He bring down fire from heaven to destroy these ingrates. How "righteous indignation" does help us let off steam! It does enable us momentarily to parole some of our imprisoned doubts, and it gives us a wonderfully expansive feeling. But it does nothing to change the situation; it may even take our minds away from the things which need to be considered and worked through. This is what was meant by Dr. Sullivan's reference to anger as "the curse of interpersonal relations!" It is a "curse" precisely because it works so well in insulating us from what is actually going on between us and others.

In our work with people it is important to remind ourselves over and over again that we all do these things in order to live. We will continue to do them as long as we are human. We all become afraid at times to ask for more information about troublesome concerns; we all compete with one another; we all rely on our status and associations to give us superiority; and at times we all lose our tempers and become angry—when we are made anxious. These are the very human and natural ways we have of living together, and they help us to bear what is sometimes an almost intolerable load. The important thing is not that we do them—but whether we can accept ourselves in the doing of them. If we can, it may be easier for us to accept others who do them too. It helps us to remember that, as we are, we are acceptable to God. Gradually, this knowledge can give us strength and support to change the unhelpful patterns of living. But it is no easy thing to have the courage, as Dr. Paul Tillich says, "to accept that we are accepted."

Jesus' Attitude to Anxiety

How did Jesus help the disciples in their anxious moments? We are told that He waited until after the day was done and they were alone together, and then He went back to some of the experiences of the day and asked them, "What were you discussing on the way?" (Mark 9:33). It would not have been very helpful to do it when the anxiety was full upon them. It was better to wait until they were alone and in the quiet of the evening. It is well to note too that Jesus did not ignore the anxiety-provoking experiences—He merely timed their consideration for a more opportune moment. Then, quietly and with understanding, He placed a child in their midst and said, "Whoever receives one such child in my name receives me" (Mark 9:37). Later He said, "Truly, I say to you, whoever does not receive the kingdom of God like a child shall not enter it" (Mark 10:15).

Jesus' method of teaching by means of parables is another example of His masterly dealing with anxious men. As He said after His parable of the sower and the seed, "He who has ears to hear, let him hear" (Mark 4:9). Later, when explaining to His disciples about this cryptic method of teaching, He gave them to understand that for some people certain insights were not bearable and, since this was so, they would take from the parable only that which they could bear. It was "so that they may indeed see but not perceive, and may indeed hear but not understand . . ." (Mark 4:12). Here we have evidence not only of Jesus' deep understanding of interpersonal relations, but of the infinite tenderness of His dealings with hurt people. We are reminded that on the night of the Last Supper He said to His disciples, "I have yet many things to say to you, but you cannot *bear** them now" (John 16:12).

When Jesus said that unless we became like little children we could not appreciate what He was talking about, could it be that He meant to encourage in us the child's attitude toward life? When a child does not understand what is going on, his very curiosity drives him to demand information and explanation. We who are parents are well aware of the annoying persistence of children at such a point. This is their way of handling anxiety—they demand to know! If our curiosity and our experience with interpersonal phenomena have not been too painful to us, we can be most helpful to them. The gaining and imparting of knowledge and understanding can be a most salutary way of helping to allay anxiety, both in ourselves and in our children.

In children do we not also see the ability to compete frankly with each other, the vying with one another for the attention of the parent? Competition among children can become quite aggressive, and it is by competition that the child begins to express one of the essential parts of his personal integrity. If competition has not been too painful for us to accept, competitive impulses and needs will not only be anxiety relieving, but also integrative in our own living. This

---

* Italics are author's.

lesson we simply must learn if we would do something in this competitive culture of ours to lighten the almost intolerable burden of guilt so many of our people bear so unnecessarily.

In the young child, we invariably see the free expression of feeling. There is no concealment with the child when it comes to the matter of feeling. Sometimes the very open expression of his resentments and his loves can be most threatening to us of more "mature" years. If it were not so threatening it might be quite refreshing to us, as well as helpful, to accept, and attempt, such honest expression of the basic impulses in our living. We in the Western culture who have discouraged the free and spontaneous expression of feelings could well learn from the Master that the way of the child is the way to Him.

Finally, if we are able to be curious, to be competitive, and to express feeling, it is almost impossible to store away or to nurse resentments or unfulfilled longings. As with the child, these feelings are out in the open, and taken care of, and no longer lie festering in the hidden recesses of the soul. It does one's heart good to see how quickly, after a bitter and violent quarrel, children will have their arms around each other and are again the best of friends, as though the storm before just had not occurred.

Jesus had a masterly way of dealing with the anxieties of men. And it seems so simple. His was an accepting and friendly attitude— a seeking to understand something of what was going on. And there is nothing that can do more to enhance and strengthen a shaky self-esteem than to know that another is so much concerned about us. This is what Jesus was like—and this is what He makes us feel God is like. This knowledge is one of the most strengthening and life-giving pastoral resources available in our ministry—if we dare share it and ourselves with our deeply troubled people.

CHAPTER SIX

LOSS *Of* FAITH
As A PASTORAL PROBLEM

"I feel as though I was losing my faith. God used to be so real to me, my faith was so beautiful, and now I'm terribly afraid of losing it." These words, spoken by a forty-eight-year-old woman who had been in the hospital for a little over a year, express vividly a problem which the pastor very frequently hears. He may not hear it in quite such dramatic language, but he certainly hears it. I shall offer some considerations which have come out of clinical experience which may prove helpful in dealing with similar difficulties.

Frequently such crisis experiences as illness exaggerate and point up more clearly what it is that has brought about this trouble. It may be, as some have already noted, that the illness is in itself the individual's attempt to solve personal difficulties which are beyond his immediate awareness. From such problem-solving experiences the discerning pastor can often learn much which will enable him to help those who are in trouble.

No Ground for Faith

I have had occasion to interview fairly frequently a patient whose background provides many illuminating insights into what led to the loss of his faith. Some of the essential facts which he related show in bold relief the importance of the emotional aspects of what might at first glance be mistaken for a purely intellectual problem.

This man was born in a foreign country. A short time before his birth, his father deserted his mother and his brother, who was then about two years old. According to the patient, his father's fear of being drafted into the army, and the attraction of the United

80

States as a land of opportunity, were sufficient to cause him to evade his parental responsibilities. When the boy was about two years old, his mother left for America to look for her husband. The patient, then an infant, was left in the care of his paternal grandparents. At about this time, his country was at war with Germany. This was during the First World War, and the patient has vivid memories of having to flee for his life and of being terrified by the cannon fire which he could hear in the distance. During this period, he found it necessary to become a beggar, going from house to house asking for food and money. He remembers having a marked conflict of feelings toward his parents. On the one hand, he hated them for their desertion, and envisioned getting even; on the other hand, he would sit for hours and "cry, and wish that I could be in my father's arms."

After the armistice, his paternal grandparents died. An aunt came to the grandmother's house where the two boys were living, and took the brother to live with her. This left the patient, who was by this time seven or eight, alone in the house with no place to go and no one to look after him.

It was about this time that the patient began to wonder what was wrong with him. He was completely shut out of everyone's life. He said he felt resentful, cynical, furious, and "an urge came over me to kill someone or to get even. But as soon as I would get these feelings, I also felt, 'Well, what's the use? Who am I to complain? Maybe I'm supposed to be left behind like this.'" After several days of his begging through the streets and coming home each night to live in the cold house, his maternal grandmother found out about the situation and came to get him. Instead of taking him to her home, she put him in an orphanage. He said, "I just wasn't able to figure out why I had to go to an orphanage, because after all I wasn't an orphan. I really had a mother and a father. And this seemed very strange to me. I used to cry." After several weeks, he ran away from the orphanage, but his grandmother returned him. He ran away again, and this time his grandmother decided to be his custodian.

The account of the next few years is rather meager in detail. We know that he was brought up in the Greek Orthodox Church, that he took his religion fairly seriously. From independent sources, it was learned that even as a child he was quite religious. When the patient was about twelve years of age, the grandparents received a letter from a cousin in America which stated that the father wanted his sons with him. The boys made the trip, only to discover that their father had not sent for them and that they were not welcome. In the meantime the father had taken a common-law wife and had three children by her. This step-mother hated the patient bitterly and tried her best to get rid of him by making things very unpleasant in the house. Not too long after his arrival in the States, the father took the boy into the city, ostensibly to visit the cousin who had written the letter. The father purchased the train tickets, gave the boy his, told him to wait on the train while he went off to get cigars, and then didn't return. He just left him.

Following this experience, the boy eventually sought for and found his mother. She had, in the meantime, obtained a divorce and remarried. She was living in a distant city with her husband, who was operating a small store. He began to work with his mother and stepfather, and soon found himself busy from early morning until late at night working in the store. This he didn't mind too much, but when he was never paid more than a pittance for his services, he became very resentful and left his mother. And from then on he was on his own.

Shortly thereafter, and at age fifteen, he met a kindly old man, an atheist, "who proved to me scientifically that there was no God." Little is known of this man, except that he was interested in the boy and sought to help him.

The subsequent history prior to the illness can be covered very briefly. These were depression years. His vocational history was spasmodic; his average wage that of a laborer. Finally, in 1934, he joined the Navy and did very well. After some years he attained the rank of Chief Petty Officer.

It is interesting to note that during this first period in the Navy he received a letter from his father stating that the step-mother had died, and if only he would come home, the father would turn the farm completely over to him. In spite of the fact that the patient had stated that he would never return home, it took him only three days to arrange for his discharge from the Navy, and be on the train home. When he arrived at his father's farm, his father fell on his neck, cried a great deal, apologized for all he had done and pleaded with him to take over the farm and to run it just as he wanted to. To the patient, however, this was like buying his affection. "It was as though my father had said to me, 'I know you think I don't love you. But here is a hundred dollars. Now, why don't you forget it?'" The mercenary attitude that he read into his father's gesture infuriated him, but the fury was never shown to his father. "The only thing I said to him was, 'No, I do not want the farm,' and that day— the very day that I arrived—I left." Apparently the patient hurt his father very deeply that day, and he states, "I just can't seem to get it out of my mind. Probably I should have taken it from the old man, but after all, I didn't want his house. I didn't want his home, I wanted a home of my own. I don't want anything from him. I want to get everything that I can on my own hook."

Shortly before hospitalization, the patient was in the Navy serving in the Pacific. He had just been promoted to the rank of Warrant Officer, over his own vigorous protestation that he did not feel qualified to carry out the responsibilities of the job. He was promoted, then, in spite of his Greek Orthodox background, married a Jewish girl after knowing her only a few days. They had met while he was on furlough. Following his marriage, he developed marked feelings of guilt as a result of sexual inadequacy in the marital relationship and his previous history of masturbation. He was hospitalized after talking about suicide. Then he made two attempts at suicide, the second one very nearly successful when he slashed his wrists and throat. He spoke very freely about this suicidal attempt. "A voice told me not to do it. If they had only trusted me, it would have been different, but I felt I was hopeless when they locked me up and put those two corpsmen to guard me. I fooled them and tried to kill myself again."

When admitted to the hospital, he greeted the chaplain with, "God has forsaken me. I'll never get well. You all know this, but you won't say it." In the same interview he spoke of himself as being an atheist, though he later added that he "believed in a supreme being." While in the hospital his relationship to the chaplain was characterized by a marked dependency. He looked forward to and sought to prolong all visits which were made, and always gave indications of needing considerable reassurance that the chaplain was going to keep his word about visiting him again. He asked for and said he read the Bible. His preferred reading in the New Testament was St. Paul's epistles to Timothy. He indicated some concern about prayer and asked to attend church. He attempted to come to church, but after only a very few visits stopped coming. He received considerable therapeutic help from the staff doctors, and after a period of six months was discharged from the hospital as improved. I do not know what has happened to him since.

I want to examine critically this material with a view toward setting forth considerations that would be of help to others who might meet the problem of the loss of faith. One of the very first considerations, and perhaps one of the most important from the viewpoint of the pastor, is that we are not dealing with a purely intellectual problem. In fact, the intellectual aspects of the problem are nearly negligible in importance. It has probably been the experience of many pastors that after having presented quite lucid reasoning against the doubts expressed by an individual, they are soon met with other doubts, and the person reiterates his feeling that his faith is gone or is going. No matter how many sound, reasonable, cogent and demonstrable arguments are produced for the existence of God, the individual's faith still remains of uncertain quality. Or, what is even worse, the person says, "You've convinced me, pastor. I don't have any doubts any longer," and finds another counselor to whom he says, "I just had to say that in order to get away from the pastor." I have heard patients tell me many times that the prayer or argument the pastor used for the existence of God didn't convince the patient. It only shut him up. He said, "I have been helped," and left to talk to somebody else.

Atheism an Authority Problem

Let us see how this is illustrated in our case. Our patient was not at all aware of the contradictions involved in his statements about being an atheist and yet at the same time believing in a supreme being. It might occur to us to dismiss this on the grounds of ignorance, but our patient was far from being ignorant. True, he had had little formal education, but his reading had made him a well-educated person. Again, it did not seem strange at all to him that he should greet the chaplain with the statement, "God has forsaken me," and yet at the same time affirm that he was an atheist. This was an "atheist" who prayed and said, as the patient put it, "Thanks, God."

This same contradiction can be demonstrated in other cases. On admission to the hospital, a brilliant doctor of philosophy gave his religion as "atheist." Now, atheists have always intrigued me. I so rarely meet an avowed atheist. This man, having a Ph.D., and having done brilliant research work, presented an excellent opportunity for me to get to know a human being who might know something of the meaning of being an atheist. So we got to talking, and I deliberately did not introduce myself. I simply came and saw him and asked him if it was all right to have an interview and went on the assumption that he would think I was a doctor or somebody other than a chaplain. I was not wearing clericals, and we got along famously for the hour. Finally I said, "Now, I'm not at all sure whether you know who I am, but I do feel that I should introduce myself. I'm a minister, I'm a chaplain here in the hospital." He froze and wanted to get out of the room. I said, "Now, just a moment. We've had a very pleasant conversation, it was very helpful to me. I've learned an awful lot. I hope it's been somewhat helpful to you. I would like to see you a few more times. I'd like, as a matter of fact, to continue this particular conversation. How do you feel about it?"

I can still see vividly his hesitancy. Then he looked to me and finally agreed. He hadn't been too traumatized. He was willing to chance a little more. And I got reasonably familiar with him.

In the first interview he discussed the subject of religion with willingness and intelligence, because he didn't know he was talking to a clergyman. After listening to him for some length and noting that he was presenting a logical and well-formed argument for the agnostic's position, I pointed this out to him. The patient replied with considerable hostile feeling that he was not an agnostic but an atheist, and it was perfectly apparent from his own observations that he knew the distinction. But he insisted on the word "atheist," and it would seem to me that the label itself has marked emotional significance.

Without going deeply into the history of this individual, what came out in our interview together was an extraordinarily complex and difficult but very hostile relationship between himself and his father. The atheists with whom I have worked have been people who have had very strong difficulty with the father-figure, and I don't think this is by any means a clinical accident. In problems of this nature, we are dealing with something that has to do primarily with the realm of the emotions. It is significant that the individual will usually present his difficulties with the words, "I feel as though I am losing my faith." To present reasonable arguments, to advance proofs of God's existence, to stress even the evidences of the belief of others is not the method of dealing with such difficulties. One can deal with them only through a frank recognition of deep-set emotional problems which require careful, patient and understanding handling. Here is where, above all, the pastor must be an observant listener, giving his parishioner the opportunity to talk and thus come to learn the facts that lie behind his present situation. Only in this manner can he offer the help that is required.

One frequently hears, when presenting clinical data obtained from those who are mentally ill, "Well, one would expect that sort of thing; these people are not normal." This is a very common conception, and it follows logically from a misapprehension of the phenomena of human conduct. There is a growing body of serious investigators of interpersonal relations who maintain that even such a marked personality disturbance as mental illness is not a matter of any difference in kind in the experiences of people, but only a difference in degree. This, of course, is Dr. Frieda Fromm-Reichmann's essential thesis. Fundamentally, we are all subject to the same laws of interpersonal activity; but through a diversity of factors (we are not all subject to the same stresses and strains) the end results in our patterns of human relations may show wide differences. But these end results are potentially present in all so-called normal activity.

Perhaps the most important consideration drawn from our material is the significance of and necessity for good personal relationships, particularly those of very early life. In the case of our patients, we have ample demonstration of poor relationships which seem to suggest a close correlation with the patient's eventual loss of faith. The first patient was deserted by his father and mother, then by his paternal grandparents (death is often interpreted by the child as the equivalent of desertion) and again by an uncle, an aunt, and finally the maternal grandparents. He appears to have had little opportunity to experience the kind of relationships to which we compare our relation to God. There was for him no real fatherly goodness, care, concern. Following the last and great rejection by his parents when he was an adolescent—and adolescence is a unique period in which the individual stands in great need of strength, support and understanding—he met the kindly old man who was an atheist. It is not surprising that he adopted the atheist's position. This rejection of religion might be more correctly interpreted as an attempt to satisfy his need for warmth and affection, since it so obviously drew him closer to this kindly old man. At the same time, we cannot overlook his rejection of the concept of God, which for him had nothing but negative and painful significance. People find meaningful only those concepts which have been demonstrated for them to have value in their living.

Loss of Faith in Self

This lack of faith in God has another side. It results in a loss of faith in one's self. When the patient was about seven or eight, at an age when he had reached some definite understanding about his experiences, he began to reflect on his being rejected so frequently. He thought, "What's the use? Who am I to complain? Maybe I'm supposed to be left behind like this." Later, when he was promoted to a higher rank in the Navy, he protested that he could not accept because he did not think he could do the job, even though he had had an extraordinarily good record in the service. Here we might draw attention to the wisdom of an ancient writer who stated that "as a man thinketh in his heart, so is he." In the patient's illness, we know that there was great preoccupation with feelings of unworthiness; he himself tells us that his nearly successful suicide attempt followed closely upon the placing of the guard over him in the hospital. " 'We don't trust you, so we guard you.' Had they trusted me, it would have been different."

One is greatly tempted here to consider suicide as the most extreme manifestation of the feeling of personal unworthiness. One hears so frequently from suicidal people the phrase, "I'm not fit to live with." It's a phrase which in itself has most meaningful implications. Certainly we can see in such people the final evidences of complete loss of self-esteem. Such a loss appears directly related to the fact that the significant people in the individual's life demonstrated to him that they had neither respect nor concern for him as a person.

It might be well for us, as pastors, to ask a parenthetical question. Of what use would it be to urge an individual like this, "thou shalt love the Lord, thy God, with all thy heart and with all thy soul and with all thy mind, and thy neighbor as thyself"? Experience has taught us that only as the individual has been able to come to terms with himself, as he has been able to settle the conflicts within himself so that he has attained some measure of healthy self-respect, can he become out-going and loving toward others. For it is only as one comes to love one's self that he is able to love others. This touches upon the insight and understanding of Jesus and of the Old Testament. This man needs not to be reminded of what he ought to do. In some measure he indicates sufficient awareness of this already. His need is to be shown the way in which this commandment can be attained. And this can never come by word only. It must come by a vital experience.

Though the patient depended so much on the chaplain, he could never trust him. I worked with him for a considerable period of time, and so did one of the psychoanalytically-oriented staff members. Between the two of us I think this man was helped, but basically he never really came to trust me. He attended very few church services: he just couldn't bear the anxiety the church itself aroused. Almost invariably, when I left the ward after clearly indicating that I was coming back at a certain time, he would go through a ritual. "You said you would come back; you promised to come back; you will not fail me."

Perhaps you were a little curious about why this man should be so much interested in St. Paul's letters to Timothy. That certainly intrigued me. (Incidentally, the Scriptures that people find most interesting are very often most revealing of their struggles.) He was most specific about his first choice of readings in the Bible. One can readily see something of why he preferred these books above others when it is remembered that the letters to Timothy were written by an old man who shows himself in his writing to be quite kindly and certainly is affectionately concerned about the young man who is beginning his life's work. His words are full of the wisdom of long experience, and his intention is to offer and to share the support and strength of careful counseling. We need hardly be reminded that these are the very things that were denied our patient in his own growing up. We have already had some indication of the light this patient's experiences can shed on well-known Scripture passages. As we become aware in some detail of such experiences in the hospital, we become even more impressed with the wisdom and the insight of the Biblical writers. Many a seminarian and clergyman who comes to study in the mental hospital becomes aware for the first time of these phenomena. The insights were there, but they were not alert to them until they had experienced these things with the patient.

Rejection by Others

In conclusion, these considerations and findings were not based merely on one individual's life experiences. Our patient happens to illustrate quite vividly what one sees also in many other individuals. In the case of the woman quoted at the beginning of this chapter, it was learned after some interviews that her faith seemed threatened at a period in her life which followed many experiences of rejection. First her father died after a lingering illness, then her husband proved unfaithful and divorced her. Some years later she became engaged again. Her fiancé died in the war, and soon afterwards her mother and sister both died. She found another suitor and he broke off the relationship with no warning. Then the patient's mother-in-law, with whom she had maintained a close relationship even after her divorce, also died. Finally, just when she became most sharply aware that the only person left who was at all close to her was her brother-in-law, he would have absolutely nothing to do with her. There followed the despairing utterance of her fear of the loss of faith. Later, in the course of working through some of these problems, she said, "My fear of the loss of someone to go to is wearing me down mentally. It is terrible when you are not wanted by your own people." She herself came to date the onset of the fear of loss of faith to the rejection by her brother-in-law.

It is recognized that this study is by no means a definitive statement of how people come to lose their faith. It is hoped, however, that the considerations which have been presented here might provide some meaningful insight which will enable us to achieve more helpful pastoral understanding and skills. These, in turn, should make it possible for us to become more effective in our pastoral opportunities.

CHAPTER SEVEN

BELIEFS THAT MATTER
In CLINICAL
PASTORAL EDUCATION

When dealing with theological considerations, a Protestant may find almost limitless latitude. When we get into the area of what clinical pastoral education *really* is we already have considerable evidence that even the experts in this field hold widely divergent views.

As a chaplain and as a supervisor, I have had a body of experience with patients, with seminary students, and with other professional workers that is seldom found in any other setting. This work has raised numerous questions as I attempted to proclaim the Good News of God as it had become personally meaningful. I think that these questions will be not only of interest but of vital concern to all in the Christian ministry. Sharing these concerns then becomes an obligation as well as a privilege.

Why Clinical Pastoral Training?

It might be well to ask *why* a hospital offers courses in clinical pastoral education. Many different answers are given by individual hospital superintendents, chaplains, institutions, depending upon the kinds of experience they have had with such programs. Here I attempt no definite answer, but I do want to offer something of what I have learned.

I feel very strongly that the mental hospital has a vast and rich body of experience that is greatly needed by the community. This covers a wide territory, but its common denominator is knowledge. In short, this is the way things are in certain kinds of living and, where this is known, something constructive might be done about one's living. Without such knowledge the inevitable difficulties of living are repeated time and time again. The hospital feels an obligation to share with community educators what it has discovered about human behavior which will in turn benefit the community at large.

The hospital is a place where the student can obtain firsthand understanding about mental illness. (What is said here applies, of course, to any progressive, therapeutically and educationally oriented institution, be it mental or general hospital, or prison.) The questions that are implicit when considering mental illness are almost limitless. Who is this person who became mentally ill? What do we know about him before it happened? What is this thing called mental illness, insofar as we can offer any general understanding? What can be done for mentally ill people to help them get well? What are the problems we run into in working with them? Above all, where does the chaplain fit into the picture? What can he do, how does he do it, what are his special understandings, if any? And, of course, not the least of the student's opportunities are his direct contacts with many psychiatrists. This forces some kind of resolution of the question, which has been quite vexing to some students, as to whether psychiatry and religion are basically opposed.

In a sense, the hospital has a twofold objective in such programs. On the one hand, it is possible to clarify and at times to eradicate frequently found misconceptions about both mental illness and psychiatry. But even more important from the hospital's viewpoint is that a great step is taken in the direction of preventing mental illness when future leaders of the community have some knowledge of what causes such illness.

The most important media of clinical pastoral education as far as the hospital is concerned are first-hand contact with patients, lectures and seminars, participation in worship and personal conferences. The goals of the chaplain-supervisor inevitably go beyond, though they are rooted in, those of the hospital. These might well be termed ultimate concerns for they focus sharply on what the clinical experience means to the student as a person. It is in this area that the theological implications of the program become apparent.

Basic Concerns Relative to Students and Programs

One of the outstanding characteristics noticed about a great many of the students when they first begin clinical training is the difficulty they have in participating personally. Being in a mental hospital is obviously a new experience for them; practically everything about the training program is an unexplored but fascinating region; and there are literally innumerable questions about everything they see and hear and do, from the very first moment they set foot in the institution. The amazing thing is their hesitancy and at times downright refusal to explore these new areas in spite of the fact that such activity is not only indicated but urged by many members of the professional staff.

Two brief examples will illustrate the point. In the first place, many of the students seem unable to show any curiosity. Some object strenuously when it is insisted in lectures or seminars that without curiosity little learning is possible. They maintain that to be curious about how the mentally ill patient came to be that way would be to show a non-Christian attitude.

Another characteristic manifestation is a pervasive dependency. This is seen in the student who constantly requests his supervisor *to tell him* what to do; whom to see; how long his visits are to be; how long to make his written interviews; what to put into his "weekly impressions sheets"; etc. It is obviously caricatured in the student who denied a patient's request for prayer with, "I can't; we haven't come to that yet in the program."

The implications of this and other characteristics will be discussed later. However, it ought to be emphasized here that many of the students who find considerable difficulty in being curious, and who tend to rely heavily on the authority of others, can and do change during the program. This change is usually evidenced in a more free and spontaneous interaction and with noticeable indications of an enhanced ability to communicate intelligibly with others.

Another aspect of this lack of personal participation is seen in the student who becomes theologically defensive. This characteristic is shown in various ways. It may be expressed by a student who criticizes his supervisor for having no theology when the supervisor refuses to be drawn into theological discussion in the process of clarifying with the student a certain student-patient relationship. One can guess at it when a student interrupts, and sometimes destroys, the communication of another student who is trying to understand what he has witnessed, by some such label as "humanism" or "logical positivism" or "liberal Christianity" or even, though more rarely these days, "social gospel."

A student who seeks to defend a theological position is often one who remains most unapproachable throughout the training. I have to admit to having learned no easy and readily usable method by which such individuals can be approached as persons.

Since the majority of theologically defensive students usually have only one year of seminary behind them, and therefore know very little theology, it is suspected that such behavior is a highly defensive maneuver to keep their personal armor intact. The ludicrousness of the position of one of our students was well illustrated one summer when a colleague rather facetiously summarized for the students what seemed to have been going on in the following words: "You are going to defend a theology which you admit you won't get until your next year in seminary, against our theology which you accuse us of never having revealed." The whole matter becomes all the more complicated—unless one views this as a defensive maneuver—when we learn, as we did from the professor of theology of the seminary from which the majority of these students came, that the following year they spent their time in his classes *defending psychiatry*.

In passing, it might be well to draw attention to the impression that students from communions (or groups within these communions) noted for their theological and liturgical *specificity* are the ones who most frequently exhibit this inhibition of personal participation.

In such training programs one frequently sees the development and expression of hostile feelings. These feelings, seen as anger or resentment or irritation, are directed usually either at the supervisory staff or at individual students, or at both. They will be voiced as a lack of confidence in the supervisor's understanding or competence or in his ability to handle group activity. Within the group, and directed at specific individuals, they may be voiced as criticisms of what another may say, questioning the motives behind certain comments, or as the open expression of anger when defenses have been directly challenged.

These feelings are not in themselves significant. What is important is that they are expressed within the group structure, where some individuals may even find themselves expressing feelings they did not know they felt. Furthermore, these very individuals happily learned that, contrary to their expectations, they were not isolated by the group. The honest sharing of feeling had resulted in a new cohesive quality which made for much more satisfying group activity.

As one would gather from the illustration just given, during the course of training a marked feeling of fellowship develops within the group. By this is not meant that everything is "buddy-buddy." Intra-group tensions are by no means eliminated. They do, however, take on a new meaning and one is able to share, in a way not possible before, vitally important aspects of living. Perhaps this is because as individuals the group members have found an acceptance which no longer keeps communication on a merely intellectual level.

Frequently toward the end of the training program one learns from students that they have found a new interest in Church doctrine and the reading of the Scriptures. Some students have been quite explicit in stating that they now were able to read the Scriptures with interest and even fascination. Doctrines which had hitherto been little more than creedal affirmations to which they were expected to give assent, suddenly presented new and enlightening perspectives on centuries-old penetrating insights on the relationship of God and man. From responses such as these one can confidently expect that the student would no longer respond to the preparation of a sermon as the "need to say something," but as a challenge to preach because "I have something to say." It is indeed a thrilling experience to be able to witness again and again the "coming alive" for a student of an ancient truth, and the liberating effect that such truth can have on hitherto moribund interpersonal relations.

One other impression about the student's reaction needs to be shared. As a result of having had the highly personal experience indicated, the student becomes rather vividly, and sometimes painfully, aware of his need to explore more deeply his interpersonal relations. With some frequency we have been called upon to arrange for students to follow up their clinical training experience with intensive psychotherapy. There is enough evidence already available that such constructive action on the part of the student, motivated because he has become aware of personal impediments in his dealings with others, has resulted in a much more effective pastoral ministry after ordination. In spite of the fears expressed in some quarters, such referral for therapy does not increase the number of students who leave the ministry. On the contrary, it appears to support the initial resolve for such a vocation and clarifies for the individual some of his more basic motivations. This leaves him less likely to express these motivations in ways unknown to himself and at the expense of his parishioners.

In all fairness, in this connection it should be added that the training experience has served another purpose. It is not unusual that students begin to have serious questions as to their motivations for entering the ministry. By and large, this has not proved too great a problem with the majority. But there have been some who, as a result of the permissive and accepting atmosphere of the program, have dared to admit that they never really wanted to be in the ministry at all. Most frequently in such cases the reasons for the original decision were the inability to withstand the demands of an aggressive mother, the unintelligent urging of an older minister or the intolerable pressure of unresolved guilts. Whenever this became clear to the student during his training period, he was helped to seek out new vocational goals. The resulting benefits to the student and his future congregations are obvious.

By and large, up to now we have concentrated on the student's reaction to training. A word should be said about the program itself and the character of the supervision offered.

In the first place, after considerable experimentation during which we moved from one end of the scale to the other, we have finally settled on a program that is rather highly structured. We have observed that the student shows considerable personal anxiety in the early phase of his training. This may be due to the newness of the experience, or his discomfort about the self-revealing aspects of the experience, or his fear of being attacked by patients, or because for the first time he is expected to be more of himself than ever had been possible before. In any case, he is anxious, and this anxiety is demonstrated in a variety of ways. It has been our experience that simply to throw the hospital, patients, staff, conferences, seminars, etc., open, with no guide-lines at all, is to induce not growth but panic in most of the students. Not in all students—just in most of them! There are some mature souls (how few they are!) who thrive on an experience like this; it is like water to a thirsty traveler. The rapidity of their growth is remarkable. But for the others, structure and direction are indispensable if there is to be any future growth.

Thus, in our programs we make some specific demands. For example, we require reports on initial religious interviews, a summary of the weekly activities of the student, and a draft of a sermon which he proposes to preach to the patients—if he elects to preach. We make it quite clear at the beginning of the program that we expect a very great deal of the student.

The program is carefully delineated as to lectures, seminars, conferences and time for patient visits or other patient activities. What the student does with this, other than in the specific demands already indicated, is up to him on very much the same basis as would be any graduate experience.

Further, in both seminars and personal conferences a considerable directiveness is offered. The student is encouraged not to ventilate personal feelings nor to simply "free associate," but to concentrate on patient or other relationships which have raised questions for him. We conceive the essence of the supervisor's function to be clarifying with the student how he relates to others. We clearly accept that we have a body of knowledge about this area of human experience which can be invaluable to the student in his future ministry, and we make a rather determined attempt to offer it to the student. However, if we find that students cannot avoid a preoccupation with personal concerns, strictly training objectives are dropped and the student is either worked with in a counseling relationship or he is referred for therapy. The values originally recognized by pioneering supervisors in "free discussion" seminars are preserved in the "group concerns" seminars. In these, as has been indicated, the student is allowed ample opportunity to discuss whatever he wants to discuss. Hence the *primary focus* of concern is always the student. But there is some acceptance of the fact that the supervisor might occasionally know something of what is going to be helpful or non-helpful to the student in his preparation for the pastoral care!

We feel strongly that it is asking too much of most students, coming as they do from an authoritarian atmosphere (be it home, college or seminary), to venture forth on their own. This is the road to panic, not learning. This is not permissiveness, but uncertain and confused supervision. It simply isn't fair to the student. In such programs, not only does the student suffer, but so does the supervisor.

Some Specific Theological Considerations

The material so far presented is replete with theological implications. The plea to view clinical pastoral training as *education,* in the real and deeply religious sense of the word, is basic. The positive affirmation of the integrity of the individual—be he patient, student, supervisor or other staff member—is stressed. Implicit is the understanding that it is not what is done *to* and *for* another, but what one is, which enables him to bring forth his latent creative and unique capacities as a "child of God . . . for whom Christ died!"

Certain theological truths are made evident by the considerations. The *spiritual emancipation of the individual* from psychological, religious dogmas, from the coercion of home and/or the supervisor, is clearly necessary if the patient is to mature spiritually *before God.* In a time when we are beset with the incessant pressures of what Rollo May has described as the "radar directed person"[1]—so sensitive to the demands of the outside world that he has become almost numb to the voice of God within—we need again to be reminded of this ancient, though double-edged truth. It requires all the wisdom and courage of deep personal certainty to meet the authoritarian demands of anxiety with the calm assurance contained

---

[1] *Man's Search for Himself* (New York: W. W. Norton & Company Inc., 1953), p. 187.

in the authority of personal witness. A deep and abiding conviction "in those things most surely believed" is required in the supervisor for him to withstand the constant temptation to violate the spiritual integrity of the student. His task has been completed when he has shared as fully as he can the deeply meaningful things of his experience—*when the student has shown evidences of being able and ready to hear such communication.* It is here that we must speak with authority—the authority of experience.

Our task as supervisors, before God, is not to persuade the student in any direction. Our solemn responsibility is to make clear to the student, most often through the wreckage of human behavior, the compelling witness of man's need for love and affection, tenderness and understanding, acceptance, reconciliation and belongingness—in short, the eternal and ever-liberating Good News proclaimed by our Lord Jesus Christ. It is our privilege to share in whatever ways we best can the spiritual realities of our own living as we carry on daily in the hospital. It is our task to do this so well that the student is left *free* to accept or reject what is offered! *This we most surely believe.*

What has been said underscores the *primacy of experience* as the basis of understanding and freedom. It is sometimes most shattering for the student to realize that when he meets patients he has literally nothing to offer *but himself.* He knows nothing of the complicated needs of the mentally ill patient. He knows not how to pray in the midst of such threatening and uncomfortable experiences. He is literally thrown back on himself. This is truly humbling, for then he has nowhere to go but to God. He has no other resource than the Ground of his Being. With understanding supervision, if his background has not been too impoverished, the student can soon come to appreciate that the greatest gift that he has to offer is the gift of himself. As he seeks through listening and patience to hear of the loneliness and suffering and pain which has been borne by the other—so he offers himself to the patient and comes to know deeply and timelessly the truth of Jesus' words, "Truly, I say to you, as you did it to one of the least of these my brethren, you did it to me" (Matt. 25:40).

It is only when the student has developed his capacity for self-awareness—when he has entered into his joys and sorrows, his loves and hates, his certainties and fears, his successes and failures—that he can truly be himself. And he can enter these life-giving experiences only insofar as he enters into relationship with others—patients, fellow students, supervisors, etc. Insofar as he does these things—which cannot be done outside of relationship—he gains experience. As he gains experience he tests the validity of his experience and increasingly plumbs the depths of his being—and cannot evade the Ground of his Being.

It is precisely when he has been encouraged to do this, and has been able to enter into it, that his new understandings concerning the Scriptures become clear. Having truly gained the *courage to be,* he is able to enter meaningfully into the being of others. With this enlightened freedom he comes to see the Holy Scriptures for what they really are—the agonizing record of man's eternal search for God; and God's unceasing quest for man—and their meeting (reconciliation) in Christ Jesus. Venturing forth into the arena of love and hate, hope and despair, salvation and sin—allowing *himself* to be what *he* is, no matter what—may be a terrifying experience, but it brings him inevitably to God. It is where we have had the courage to see the flesh—where we have had the courage to be flesh—to see ourselves clearly, steadily and as a whole—that we meet God. The Word indeed became flesh and dwelt among us, for God was in Christ reconciling us unto Himself. *This we most surely believe.*

This brings us to another great truth—that the individual is made whole only insofar as he has *become at one with God.* This has been perhaps most meaningfully expressed for us in the saying that we are "justified by our faith." Not by what we do or say—not by a formula or methodology—but by a living relationship with a living Being. "Man does not live by bread alone, but by every word that proceedeth out of the mouth of God." It is where we have found acceptance, where our deep dignity in striving toward God is recognized, no matter what we may *show,* where we have found a new relationship, that we become whole, or are saved. This can be only where we have known patience, consideration, friendliness, concern—somebody reaching out seeking to know something of what has happened to us—where indeed the understood Truth of the Ages—the Word—becomes flesh!

What does this mean in everyday experience? Many things, of course! But not the least of these is knowing that we are accepted before God as we are. We are sure that we do not have to give up part of ourselves before we come to know love. We even dare to believe that we can come "Just as I am . . . ," *sin and all*. God does not require that we give up our sin before we come to Him. It is our glory and triumph that He wants us and needs us, sin and all. Indeed, our sinful nature being what it is in some peculiar way makes us what we are—and this is what we have to offer to God. It is our strong feeling that as Christians we are never truly asked to give up our sinful natures—but to give them to God. "In his service we find perfect freedom." When we again remember that *before God* Jonah is reported to have spat out the words, "I do well to be angry," and suffered no rebuke; and that Our Lord Himself on the Cross— *before God*—could accusingly cry, "My God, my God, why hast Thou forsaken me . . ." and yet receive an Eternal Acceptance from the Father—then we know that there is indeed "nothing that can separate us from the love of God which we have seen in Christ Jesus." When we are in the hospital such experience and such truth are inescapable. When we are truly ourselves we know that we are accepted before God. *This we most surely believe.*

Now to point to but one more great truth validated by our experience. It has already been mentioned that clinical pastoral training gives the group a remarkable sense of fellowship. Sometimes this is so strong that, when a reasonably large group of students in a given center come from a single seminary, they often go back to the seminary and make an attempt to retain some of the group life they had during the summer—to the discomfiture of other students and faculty alike. This testifies not only to the vitality of the experience, but to the inherent need we all have to share together, and *in community,* the deeply significant things of human living. Such is the essence of fellowship.

We have long known about the Church as a holy community or as the fellowship of believers. Our experience underscores the truth of this ancient witness concerning the Body of Christ, and bears testimony to the reality of this experience. When a group meets together for a common purpose, to know something about another area of human living, and members share the feelings involved in this new exploration, there is indeed a new creation. Something unique has happened—account for it as you will. When the individuals of this group come together not only to know about this new area of experience, but in relationship to the Ultimate which is devoutly and most certainly believed—and affirm this in terms of the living faith of the Lord Jesus Christ—then the Body of Christ is alive. Where we seek to share some of the inevitable pain of life, face together our separation, loneliness, and longing—to find the meaning of life as He revealed His Touch to us,—we are met together in *His name*. And there He is also! *This we most surely believe!*

Interestingly enough, where a group has achieved unity, the fact that various members of the group represented Baptist, Lutheran, Presbyterian, Methodist, Episcopal persuasions did not hinder the essential oneness achieved. Rather it enriched it! This points to a new hope for ecumenicity. Clinical training is a unique and meaningful experiment in ecumenicity.

This means that prayer takes on new meaning, as do worship, the sacraments, the liturgical symbols of the ages, in fact all the rich treasures we have inherited. These can no longer be accepted with mere formality. Having thrown off the shackles which have bound our individual creativity we can no longer be satisfied until we have entered fully into these joyful mysteries.

I am mindful of the implications of an ancient truth—that there is nothing definitive about what has been said, but at least it does not remain unsaid. If there is anything needed in the theological realm today, it is the reformulation of ancient truth in the light of psychological understanding. All else—and there is much of it—is, to use a phrase from the Bishop of Birmingham—"Clever and sterile thought coming from tiresome specialists . . . (and) makes no appeal to men and women of modern education sick at heart with the dangers and perplexities that surround them."[2] There is, of course,

---

[2] Ernest William Barnes, "Religion and Turmoil" (The Rede Lecture, given at Cambridge University, 1949), p. 36.

one understanding exception to this—Dr. Paul Tillich, who has had the courage to say in his autobiographical reflections: "I do not think that it is possible today to elaborate a Christian doctrine of man, and especially a Christian doctrine of the Christian man, without using the immense material brought forth by depth psychology."[3]

Only as we pool our common experiences and share our uniqueness as individuals through a deep and humble conviction of the truth we have *lived,* in a common bond of fellowship that gives us courage to affirm ourselves, can we fully enter into the divine truth which has been given us. This we need—and this is demanded of us by the very perplexities of our age.

---

[3] Charles W. Kegley and Robert W. Bretall, eds., *The Theology of Paul Tillich* (New York: The Macmillan Company, 1952), p. 19.

CHAPTER EIGHT

PSYCHIATRY
OPENS The DOOR

There is a great deal of interest in the relationship of psychiatry and religion today. Why should this be so? It is inevitable that we ask the question, but not so easy to provide the answer. Surely the clue might be found in the general anxiety of our times. Everywhere there is confusion and unrest. Never in the history of mankind have we been promised so much—even attained so much—and yet found ourselves so wanting. The haunting fact remains that our lack has come not as a result of what we need from the world about us but from the impoverishment of our spirit. Ours is a day when standing in the midst of plenty we are starved. As we have come to recognize even though dimly, that the causes of this starvation lie within man rather than in nature, so we have come to doubt whether there is anything in which we can believe, anything in which we can place our trust. This bankruptcy of the soul provides fertile ground for those who are deeply concerned with the fundamental issues of man's existence. It is only natural then that we should turn to those two disciplines which have had the most extensive and intensive experience in dealing with deeply troubled people.

The Question of Conflict. Perhaps the first thing which comes to our minds when we talk about psychiatry and religion is the conflict which is said to exist between these two disciplines. Unfortunately, much of what has been said about this "conflict" has tended only to confuse rather than to clarify the issue. However, there are increasing signs that this "conflict" has lessened considerably within the past decade. This has come about largely as a result of the determined efforts of people in each discipline who have patiently tried to understand the basic concerns held to be important by the other profession. Here the clinical pastoral training of ministers has done a very great deal to help resolve some of the uncertainties shared by both disciplines.

However, among the clergy there is still much concern because psychiatry is considered to be anti-religious. Ever since Sigmund Freud published his views on religion, many have feared lest religion have no more future than an illusion. However, the criticism which Freud leveled at religion in his *Future of an Illusion* has been ably met by competent experts in the field of psychiatry itself. Dr. Gregory Zilboorg in *Mind, Medicine and Man* points out that, in his criticism of religion, Freud was allowing himself a most unscientific generalization from the only particulars with which he was acquainted. In short, you cannot condemn all religion or all religious experience just because certain people with whom you have worked have found their experience with religion more crippling and destructive than strengthening and life-affirming. It might well be that many ministers would find the areas of so-called "conflict" between religion and psychiatry almost non-existent if they could be reminded that such "conflicts" are most often a commentary on the personalities of practitioners rather than on the disciplines they represent.

If there were time available, one could present many convincing arguments that religion and psychiatry are not really opposed to each other. Yet neither are the two disciplines necessarily allies. Since they have in common the same ground of operation, the soul of man, they can at least be complementary. When practitioners of these two disciplines respect the integrity and worth of the individual soul, and demonstrate this in their practice, there need be no conflict between them.

It is relatively easy to see why, from the psychiatrist's viewpoint, these two disciplines are unalterably opposed, if the psychiatrist accepts the dogmatic generalizations of Sigmund Freud uncritically. It is equally easy to see why the religionist finds a contradiction if he makes a similar mistake: that is, if he accepts the authoritarian position of some religious leaders whose basic premise is that the individual must be made subordinate. But, as is the case with any extremes, the truth of the matter lies with neither. Now that the smoke of many of our verbal and pen battles has begun to lift, we are coming to see the issue more clearly.

Again, concern has been expressed because the psychiatrist is so frequently reported to be of more help than the clergyman to deeply troubled people. This is altogether too true, and is pointed up for us by the study mentioned earlier.[1] People in trouble do first turn to the clergyman for help, but (as the study also indicated) they are all too often disappointed in the kind of help they get. We, the clergy, have simply not been as helpful as our people have a right to expect.

There is good reason why this is so. First, we in the clergy have not received, as has the psychiatrist, adequate training to prepare us for our work with individuals, though much more emphasis is being given to this today. But, there is a second and equally important consideration. There has been too much preoccupation with the preaching of moralistic sermons which are condemnatory and critical, and from which the average person is able to obtain little more than an increase of guilt and inferiority feelings. The help a troubled person needs so badly cannot come from such sermons.

Illustrative of this is an incident that happened not long ago. A radio station was broadcasting a transcription of a bitter sermon. Suddenly the preacher's voice was heard to say over and over, "God's damnation . . . God's damnation . . . God's damnation . . ." until somebody finally came and lifted the needle out of the groove. It would be helpful if we were to face the fact that many of us *have* been stuck in the groove of a negative and guilt-increasing type of preaching!

There is a more hopeful side. Today there has come to be a rather marked concern that the theological student in his preparation for the ministry be given training in work *with* people. Books and theory, whether the theory be theology or not, are simply not enough!

Some Contributions of Psychiatry to Religion

The Concern for the Individual: Respect for His Unique Integrity. Perhaps the emphasis in psychiatry of major interest to religion is a concern for the individual and respect for his unique integrity as a person. This is a most welcome note in a day when

---

[1] See Preface, page 14.

mass-production, extensive activity and the preoccupation with crowds have made it most difficult for us to see people as individuals.

The psychiatrist's concern starts with the individual *as he is.* This is reflected in the questions which are in the mind of the doctor as he begins working with the patient: "What is the patient trying to tell me about his trouble? How did he come to be the way he is? What purpose does this illness serve him? How can he be helped to face life so he will no longer need to rely on the unhelpful personality responses which are crippling his relations with others?" In such an approach to the patient one seldom finds the attitude which suggests that the patient is "bad" because he does what he does, that he "ought to know better," that he "should exert himself," or even worse, "what would your mother think of you now?"

Such an understanding approach on the part of the psychiatrist obviously indicates a concern for the integrity of the patient's personality. It spells out that concern in such a way that the patient is never told what to do, though he is led to see for himself what is helpful and non-helpful in his living. Above all, he is given a great deal of time to talk over the things which have been so difficult for him. Listening to the patient has been one of the life-saving factors in any doctor-patient relationship. In such a relationship the patient, perhaps for the first time in his life, expresses what he really feels without encountering a negative or condemnatory attitude on the part of the listener. To make it possible for him to do this, the doctor very clearly conveys to him that he knows the patient never wanted to be as he now is, and is not satisfied with what he has become, but that he has never really been helped to see himself as he is. Just such an approach has given many a patient the strength to do something with his own abilities and personality resources. As a result, the patient is able to confront his past failures in living, deal with his present inadequacies, and plan realistically for the future. He no longer has to live his life in a fragmentary manner, for he has been helped to achieve a wholeness or health which has come to be his salvation.

The Basic Drive of the Personality Is Always Toward Health. That the basic drive of the personality is always toward health does not mean that we can be too optimistic about human nature. Such a statement might be thought to imply the dangerous fallacy, "Leave man to himself, and he will surely find his way to heaven." This is not what is meant! Man's present confusion, the chaos of his personal and international life, are all too present and discordant notes to be alleviated by any such sweet symphony. By himself, man is often a bewildered and all too blind fumbler in the area of interpersonal relations. But true as that may be, it does not invalidate the observation that man is endowed with tremendous life-giving potentialities and that these inevitably drive him on toward health.

So, we come to the second major psychiatric formulation: that the basic drive of the individual is always toward health. It is a matter of real significance that the psychiatrist should come to this conclusion. After all, he works constantly in the area of human distress. He is daily confronted with the negative factors in human living. It is his task to deal with the failures people have experienced in living with one another and with themselves. It is out of just such experiences that this proposition has developed. Such living human testimony can neither be silenced nor ignored. It is the sick person, the emotionally disturbed individual, the defeated human being who, having been given even a modicum of attention, support and understanding from one not involved in his illness, has shown remarkable changes in living. No doctor gives himself the credit for having "cured" the patient, for the doctor is too well aware of his own limitations. But what he would probably say is this, that he helped remove the obstacles in the way of the patient's living and the patient "cured" himself. We might add, "It was God who gave the cure, God who is the source of life and its inevitable drive toward the positive and the good," and we would be right!

Surely it is not a surprise to us that there should be so emphatic a pronouncement from the psychiatrist: that the basic drive of the personality is toward health. The only surprise might be that such words have come to us from a profession many of us have mistakenly believed was both negative and pessimistic in its view of man. To us who have believed in the Doctrine of the Holy Spirit, who have accepted the teaching of Saint Paul that we are the Temple of the Holy Spirit, this should be no new understanding. Could it be that our own failures in living have tended to dim our faith so that we no longer dare trust the infinite potentialities with which God, our Father, has endowed us?

Psychiatry's Emphasis on the Need for a New Relationship. If what has been said so far has any validity, then it must follow that in order to find ourselves we must experience a new relationship. This is the third great contribution of psychiatry we might consider.

If our awareness of ourselves as unique creations of God and of the almost limitless resources we have in ourselves for health and life have become for us nothing more than theory and the sound of fine words, then we need a new and vital relationship with another. This is what psychiatry has amply demonstrated many times. This is what our religion has always proclaimed to be the essence of its message. Our Lord said: "I am the way, and the truth, and the life." "I am the door, by me shall ye enter in." "I came that they might have life, and that they might have it more abundantly." It is significant that this new life appeared to have come to those who followed Him not through anything new He taught, but out of a relationship, a new relationship, which they were able to achieve—*and with Him!* This remains true to this day. New life must inevitably come out of an experience of acceptance we have from another. We call this love—so it is! From love comes life! It is only when we are accepted as we are that we gain the courage to attain a new life.

There is infinite tragedy in the fact that the glorious good news of the new relationship which we can find with one another and with our God has remained for many of us nothing more than verbalization. We have never quite managed to get beyond the listening to, or the preaching of, fine sermons about how good God is—sermons which often leave us a little irritated, and a little guilty about the feeling. From all this one painful fact emerges quite clearly, deny it as we will: unless we have known somebody from whom we have experienced love, somebody who reached out and accepted us as we were, somebody who sought to help us when we most needed help, all else remains little more than the sound of fine words.

This again is not new. We are told by the writer of the Epistle of Saint John that "we love because he first loved us." We can interpret this to mean that we are able to love because we have first been loved. The converse follows: we are unable to love unless we have first been loved. Without the hope that we shall be loved, that we shall know and be known in actual living human experiences, none of us could live. This was known to the Psalmist who wrote, "I should utterly have fainted but that I believe verily to see the goodness of the Lord *in the land of the living*" (Ps. 27:13, *The Book of Common Prayer*).* In the land of the living . . . that I would still come to know something of the warmth and friendliness of human tenderness. If it were not so, I would utterly have perished.

It would be easy to point to Jesus as having demonstrated that new relationship. Out of his experience he was (as *The Book of Common Prayer* puts it) "bold to say, *Our Father* . . ." That is because out of his living he had come to know that one could trust, rely on, believe in, have confidence in God as a Father. But we must come to know this relationship for ourselves, from our own living.

How can we know it? We gain the experience through a considerate friendliness: through coming to feel understanding, interest, concern, helpfulness in our relations with each other. We talk about the things which are important to us so that we can rid ourselves, at least in part, of the horrible loneliness which we have tried to hide, and so that we can be ourselves, just as we are, with others who really matter to us. There is no other way. This, we dare to believe is what God is like with us. He accepts us as we are. He does not even ask us to give up our sins before we dare approach Him. Once we know Him, the radiance of the new life with Him works to make us stronger. We need no longer depend upon the unhelpful and inadequate patterns that we have previously used to hobble our crippled way through life. This is what deeply troubled people long to know!

This has been, at best, a very brief outline of some of the distinctive emphases of psychiatry which might interest the minister: the sacredness of the individual personality; the unlimited possibilities for

---

* Italics are author's.

new life in all, "created in the image of God, children of the living God"; and the need for a new relationship by which we can grow into the new life we believe God has divinely intended for us all. These are religion's fundamental concerns.

Psychiatry cannot give us these goals. They are our inalienable right. They are God-given. Psychiatry can only help us to appreciate them, to see them a little more clearly by helping to remove the obstacles in the way of their attainment. For this, psychiatry uses the same tools which we as ministers must use: concern for others, concern for them *as they are,* not a moralistic concern, but a friendly, helpful concern. This is an attitude which can recognize that we, too, have often been as hurt and fearful as they are, as bewildered as they have become, but that even in such a situation we have known the acceptance and Love of God, and dare to believe that He has received us as we are. Then we can say that the truth has made us free, and our love has overcome our fear.

CHAPTER NINE

PSYCHOTHERAPY
As A MEANS
To WHOLENESS

What makes a man religious? Dr. Albert Schweitzer trenchantly
says that religion is "reverence for life," and he appears quite willing
to leave it at that. This is a magnificent concept; perhaps we could
attain some real ecumenicity if this were the cardinal principle and
we had spent some considerable time investigating its profoundness.
However, some elaboration here would be helpful.

We must begin with reverence for life! To be religious is to
have a profound feeling for the present in terms of the ultimate; and,
by action and perhaps by verbalization, to indicate the recognition
of that which is beyond the self. To this would certainly next be
added the ability to trust others and that which is beyond one's self
as having integrated meaning. And, our ability to trust others implies
that we have trust in ourselves—we "accept ourselves as acceptable,"
to use Dr. Paul Tillich's fine phrase. Finally, these attitudes must
have become so much a part of ourselves that we avail ourselves of
the best insights and practices of our respective vocations so that we
may offer others the best that we know. Surely it is in these four
emphases that we find the qualities of a religious man.

Now, let us come to psychotherapy. Here Dr. David E. Roberts,
author of *Psychotherapy and a Christian View of Man*, has done us
a real service in his chapter on "How Therapy Works and Why."[1]
This volume is well worth reading and rereading.

What is psychotherapy? It is that process which goes on between
two people whereby new understandings and abilities are gained
directly as a result of what both contribute to the relationship. To

---

[1] David E. Roberts, *Psychotherapy and a Christian View of Man* (New
York: Charles Scribner's Sons, 1950), Chapter III.

it the therapist brings his training and understandings; the patient brings his experience in living—the very problems that make it difficult for him to function. The curative effects come about largely through the process of verbal and non-verbal communication, allowing the patient to achieve greater responsibility, creativity, and spontaneity in his living. What makes this process psychotherapy is the quality of understanding and relationships which the therapist (be he a doctor, psychiatrist, psychoanalyst, or whatever) is able to demonstrate as a result of his own experience, training, and understanding. It can as easily be done by a clergyman as by a physician, but probably will not be, largely because pastoral training provides so few opportunities for gaining the experience and understandings which are indispensable.

It has long been recognized that the key factor in therapy is the relationship which exists between therapist and patient—the transference relationship—and that the understanding and handling of this relationship determines the success or failure of the treatment. There are wide differences in what this relationship is conceived to be, and in the various concepts we see reflected the conflicting theories of the various "schools" in psychoanalysis. But, our concerns definitely center in the quality of this relationship and what the patient and therapist together are able to make of it.

The New Birth

I would like now to quote from an article which has been of real help in my understanding of this very difficult field. I refer to Dr. Janet M. Rioch's "The Transference Phenomenon in Psychoanalytic Therapy."[2]

> Psychoanalytic cure is not the amassing of data, either from childhood, or from the study of the present situation. Nor does cure result from a repetition of the original injurious experience in the analytical relationship. What is curative in the process is that in tending to reconstruct with the analyst that atmosphere which ob-

---

[2] Janet McKenzie Rioch, "The Transference Phenomenon in Psychoanalytic Therapy," *Psychiatry: Journal of the Biology and Pathology of Interpersonal Relations*, Vol. VI, No. 2 (1943).

tained in childhood, the patient actually achieves something new. He discovers that part of himself which had to be repressed at the time of the original experience. He can only do this in an inter-personal relationship with the analyst, which is suitable to such a re-discovery.

The two main points stressed here deserve special consideration. In the first place, one cannot emphasize too much that "something new" comes about as a result of this therapy. In short, the repressed parts of the personality—the parts that had to be disavowed because they were unacceptable to the self, probably because they were unacceptable to others who were important to the individual—are regained and made available to him. (It is important to remember here that not all of what is repressed by the individual is either asocial or destructive in nature. We can witness here to the most difficult time our Western culture seems to be having with feelings of warmth and tenderness which are frequently repressed to the consequent impoverishment of the personality.) And then the second main point: that this "something new" is attained by the individual as a direct result of the attitude of the therapist. That is, what the therapist is in and of himself, what he has experienced (dare we say, what he is able to trust?) determines whether or not the dissociated experiences of the past are to be regained.

For the religious worker, concerned as he is with the quality of relationships, this is of unusual significance. It says in essence that the character of the therapist and what his attitude is determines in the last analysis what he is able to create out of the relationship.

At this point attention must be drawn to Dr. Carrol Wise's volume on *Pastoral Counseling*. Here we see cogently stated the importance of the counselor's basic attitude. It is only when the pastor has been able to come to terms with his own experience in living, his successes and failures, his joys and sorrows, that he can appreciate and help deal with, rather than be threatened by, similar experiences of others. I like the phrase Dr. Wise uses: "The central problem of the pastor is not what he does for people, nor yet what he does to people, but what he IS to people."[3] This is of paramount significance.

---

[3] (New York: Harper & Row, Publishers, 1951).

It may be helpful to point out here, even though parenthetically, that such emphasis throws considerable light on our understanding of the nature of sin. If we see sin as basically our separation from God, and from our neighbor as well as from ourselves, then we are reminded vividly that what we have to repress through fear and to maintain in a state of dissociation equally produces a feeling of isolation. For, after all, these things have been repressed because they have been "bad," bad in our relationship with others, even though intrinsically there may have been nothing wrong and probably much that was right with what had to be repressed.

Isolation Equals Guilt

It would seem to me then that this would also illuminate an ancient Biblical observation: that the mentally ill that Jesus met were most definitely upset whenever He came into contact with them. This is characterized by such questions as "What have you to do with us, O Son of God? Have you come here to torment us?" (Matt. 8:29). If mental illness is synonymous with massive dissociation of large segments of our personality, and this has come about because we could not admit these segments with their threatening implications as being part of ourselves, then it is to be expected that there will be a marked sense of isolation on the part of the individual and a consequent feeling of guilt. This has been called by such experts as Dr. Erich Fromm and Dr. Anton T. Boisen the crux of the problem of mental illness. It is also what one finds frequently to be the problem of the mentally ill patient in the hospital. Here it is graphically expressed as "What I had feared has finally happened: I have always thought that I was the kind of a person (bad) who ought to be made to come to a place like this (a place of known social stigma)!" In particular, this accounts for Søren Kierkegaard's brilliant observation with regard to the "demoniacal" (mental illness) as "shut-up-ness unfreely revealed," and his definition of anxiety as "the dread of the good."[4]

It has been suggested that one of the original meanings of the word "religion" has to do with the "re-tying or re-uniting" of man's

---

[4] Kierkegaard, *The Concept of Dread*, Chap. 4.

experience—that, in fact, all that religion is and does seeks to obtain an integration of experience. This would imply that it is possible for the personality to become disintegrated, for parts of one's experience to be carried about with little or no reference to other parts; that the past often is at variance with the present, and that both are at considerable odds at the prospects of the future. This, of course, is psychologically demonstrable.

Perhaps we have been puzzled by some people who so effectively (it seems) compartmentalize their lives. This is what they appear to have done. It is here that the depth psychologist's understandings are of marked significance. The psychoanalyst says in effect: "Much of what has happened to most of us as the inevitable concomitant of our being human and living together has been so unacceptable to those with whom we were brought up and who were very important to us, that we have repressed that part of our living." Consider the so-called "barren years" before the individual becomes five years of age. These years are anything but barren! In fact, they are replete with aggressive and erotic interests. This may be one of the reasons why they are so painful to remember. As a result of these experiences our personalities are in real need of "re-tying"; that is, we have to bring together the past and the present so that we can make constructive plans for the future.

The Antidotes to Fear

How then is this to be done? Surely not everybody must be analyzed. Of course not, but what we all need, some more than others, is to be able to confront ourselves in an atmosphere of acceptance, an atmosphere that is different from the one that made us "shy off" from the experiences which came to be repressed. This atmosphere can best be suggested in such descriptive language as satisfying the individual's need for friendliness, understanding, concern, warmth, and tenderness, permissiveness, outgoingness, and patience; or, as fostering relationships with others which include no condemnation, blame, or hostile criticism. These are the things that Saint Paul talked about so magnificently in his thirteenth chapter of I Corinthians when he spelled out the meaning of love. These attitudes are the antidotes of fear!

The Bible speaks much about fear (in the sense of anxiety) and the need to deal constructively with it. The references to it would be well worth exhaustive study. We see the concern with anxiety quite vividly expressed, even though symbolically, in the angelic visitation at the time of the Nativity. Here the first words spoken are "Fear not . . ." which is surely a strange note with which to announce such glorious good news. Does this not indicate a profound awareness that what the incarnation attempts to deal with basically is this fundamental of the human situation? One cannot sing "Gloria in Excelsis . . ." until one has first been helped to deal with one's fear. Saint John poignantly reminds us "perfect love casts out fear" (I John 4:18).

Only in an atmosphere where one feels love in the sense described above—where one feels accepted—can the past be confronted and made part of one's everyday experience in living. For it is in being able "to accept acceptance" that we deal constructively with the anxiety which Dr. Harry Stack Sullivan described as "that which one experiences as a threat to one's sense of self-esteem." It is this anxiety which all too often one unhelpfully attempts to deal with by confusing and restricting one's awareness of what is going on.

This presents no end of intriguing possibilities to the religious worker. Here he is brought up short with the very basic questions of his religious affirmation. What is God like? What is my relationship to Him? What is the reason for my existence? These are the questions with which our Lord tried to deal constantly in His daily experience with men.

The first thing which stands out is His relationship to God. It is to me most singularly interesting that we see such a marked contrast between Saint John the Baptist's attitude toward God (as reflected in his preaching) and the attitude of our Lord. For example, in the first chapter of Mark, "John came preaching *repentance* . . . Jesus came preaching the *good news** of God's love and understanding and forgiveness." John started with man's failure—sin—and caustically called his hearers a "generation of vipers." His was a condemnatory kind of preaching! Jesus started with an affirmation of God's love and concern—that we all are God's children, that He is

---

* Italics are author's.

our loving, forgiving Father, that we have indeed all gone astray, are indeed all in need of help—but God wills not the destruction of any, "but that all might be saved."

This distinction is not one of basic interpretation—it does not mean that John was and Jesus was not concerned with man's sin! It is a distinction of emphasis—John started with it (and presumably scared people to death); Jesus ended with it, after people had been won to Him through understanding.

Jesus then teaches us that, by what He knew of the nature of God, we can go to Him in perfect confidence of being accepted as we are. Indeed it is written, "While we were yet sinners Christ died for us" (Rom. 5:8). So it is implied that we are not asked to give up our sin before we come to God, but that we come to God, sin and all, and He accepts us as we are. Having known such love, in that new relationship, we shall find that the old unhealthy patterns upon which we have relied will no longer be such necessary crutches. In that new relationship we shall be able to rely more on ourselves because we have come to rely on Him. It will indeed be as Irenaeus put it, "He became as we are in order to make us as He is."

Martin Luther points up how important it is that we have such a trust in God. He followed John Gerson in advising an occasional missing of confession before Holy Communion just so that the "sinner" might be reminded that he was welcome before God just as he was—as Luther puts it so beautifully, "not missing the sacrament in order to despise it or to tempt God, but only in order that you may accustom a troubled conscience to trust in God and not to tremble at the rustling of every falling leaf."[5]

What happens to us, then, as a result of this new atmosphere which we experience "in Christ Jesus"? Through it we shall find the courage to look back at what we have been, where we have been, what we have done, and we shall find sufficient strength to deal constructively with these experiences. We shall be able to absorb the helpful because it is helpful, and slough off the unhelpful elements of human living simply because they are unhelpful, and not because we fear the loss of love or the loss of self-esteem. By this very pattern

---

[5] *A History of the Cure of Souls*, John T. McNeill (New York: Harper & Row, Publishers, 1951), p. 167.

our self-esteem can increase because we are basically validating the very integrity of our beings.

How shall we describe this? If we have been able to bring back into awareness that which had been formerly lost to us, if we are able now to utilize past experiences, if we are no longer at war with ourselves, then we can say that we have found at least a measure of "wholeness." If we are in fact "at one" with ourselves (our experiences and feelings), then we can say we are in that sense "healthy." It is believed that the Church has always taught this as the direction of salvation. Our salvation is rooted in our at-oneness with God and ourselves.

Faith and Practice

Since it is so important that we have an atmosphere in which the past can be helpfully (integratively) dealt with, how does the Church help us attain this? Here we are confronted with the distinctive contribution of the Church down through the ages—the faith and practice which has been handed down as our sacred heritage. In brief, it might be put this way: By what the Church teaches (its faith) and by what the Church does (its practice) have men found salvation for their souls. Of course this is not intended in a restrictive, coercive, and dogmatic fashion—"this believe and this do or be damned"—but rather as an informative or declarative statement: "By this shall ye live." In all honesty it must be admitted that the history of Christianity has much in it to disprove this statement. Note the strongly coercive element in "The Creed of Saint Athanasius"— "which faith except a man keep whole and undefiled; without doubt he will perish eternally!"

What, then, can be said about the "faith" of the Church? By "faith" I mean not only the things taught—those values found integrative and helpful in human living—but the very attitude or "trust" by which they are derived and by which they become part of our daily lives. Here we might go into great detail for in this area we are concerned with the nature of God, the nature of Christ, the nature of man, the nature of salvation, the nature of the Church, the purpose and meaning of existence, and the ultimate destiny of man. What do these concepts mean from the point of view of the therapist?

Here we come to the truth in Jung's frequently quoted observation that ultimately cure is found only when the individual has attained a sense of meaning and purpose in life. I am reminded of a statement by an officer who came through South Pacific combat duty in World War II without "combat fatigue" while many of his companions cracked up. Asked how he had managed to escape, his answer was, "I am a Harvard man." Another officer in serious difficulty on the battlefield in Europe, when his own life as well as the lives of others depended on his achieving obedience to his commands, swore, "I will shoot to kill just as sure as I am a West Point man." He often wondered why he had to drag in West Point in that situation. It appears obvious: When we have a tradition, a faith which we accept, a faith which gives meaning and purpose, it offers a stability to our living not found otherwise. Especially is this so in crisis situations. The teaching of the Church, the teaching of her faith, gives stability and sense of direction to us when we are most confused about our meaning and purpose in the world. Let us make no mistake about this. Not one of us can ever evade the "meaninglessness of life," as Tillich so trenchantly points out; it must be not denied but embraced. The anxiety attendant upon it must be accepted for what it is if the individual is to be truly Christian and is to find integration.

What we have been saying here in effect is this: The psychologist tells us that without a faith we cannot really live. We all must believe (in the sense that it is our need, not that we are compelled from outside ourselves and by others)—we must believe in something. What the Church seeks to provide in the faith it offers is a reasonably intelligent interpretation of the fundamental values by which man lives.

This of course presents other problems. This faith—"theology," if you will—needs constant revision. There is nothing sacrosanct about it; it is an attempt to deal rationally with man's experience, and if it is to do so it must change as man's understanding of himself and his experience changes. Here we run into a real hurdle! To make such changes demands real emotional security, security within, because making changes obviously implies that our understandings are limited. To people who are made doubly insecure by the vicissitudes of their everyday living recognition of this is well-nigh impossible and may account for the hegira to the fascistic or communistic—that is, *authoritarian*—philosophies or religions with which we are recurrently plagued. It may explain in some measure why so many of us find no real "security" until we have made our "escape from freedom" into the dogmatic atmosphere of an affirmation which tells us to accept only that which has been thought out for us.

One last point needs to be made. Important as it is to have "faith" or understanding about the values of life, and necessary as this is to build up a "trust" (faith *is* trust) about life, it is equally important that such a faith (even with all its intellectual acumen) becomes vitiated when it is forced upon an individual. We can "evangelize" the world by offering "the good news" through our own understanding and its basic meaning for ourselves, and leave it to others to accept it on that basis. Thus we demonstrate that what we hold dear has value, not because we or others say it has value, but because it has meaning in existence or in function.

Now we must of necessity deal for a moment with the application of the religious faith just mentioned. Here we enter into what we might well call the "practice" of the Church, what the Church has done through the years to make real her faith. Here we are confronted with the rich resources of the Church—worship, prayer, sacraments, preaching—all of which are part of the larger whole which we call the fellowship of the Church. It is by and through the fellowship that the faith of the Church becomes alive and meaningful. It is in the fellowship—in the "group experience" to which the individual comes *as he is* ("while we were yet sinners . . .")—that he finds his acceptance. This gives him the security to go on and obtain *for* himself what he is unable to attain *by* himself. In essence, the fellowship is that group experience which provides by togetherness for the exchange of experience and the sharing of common goals, aspirations, fears, joys, sorrows, failures and successes!

It is in this fellowship that we gain the courage (Paul Tillich's "faith") or the daring "to accept that we are accepted." For in fellowship, if you are *in* and remain so no matter what you do or say, you experience this quality of acceptance.

As an example of this we might draw attention to the experience of one of our students in clinical training. This student was usually a quiet and reserved individual who took little active part in the group experiences. But one day he "blew up" at one of the members of the group and expressed himself forcefully. He was amazed and overwhelmed at his action. However, the other young men in the group stated that they now felt for the first time that they really knew him as a person and that they liked him. Thus, this sharing of negative feelings provided an integrative experience, but precisely because it was in an atmosphere where he was accepted. This student also obtained new insight into the Prayer of Consecration in the Holy Communion Service where the celebrant says: "And here we offer and present unto Thee O Lord our selves, our souls and bodies, to be a reasonable Holy and living sacrifice . . ." As he said in a conference later, "I used to feel in this prayer that what I could offer to God was only the good in me, but as a result of this summer's experience I learned that it was possible to find a new life by also sharing with others my resentments and disagreements. I now know that these are just as acceptable to God as were my other experiences, and in the group fellowship that has meant new life." One wonders whether this does not testify to the validity of Martin Luther's observation in the *Babylonian Captivity*,[6] when he says, "For when we have laid bare our conscience to our brother and privately made known to him the evil that lurked within, we receive from our brother's lips the word of comfort spoken by God Himself; and if we accept it in faith, we find peace in the mercy of God speaking to us through our brother." It is indeed gratifying to see, as we almost invariably do in each clinical pastoral training group, a number of students finding a new meaning in fellowship when they were able to share some of their honest feeling.

Much more could be and should be said about the relationship of theology and psychotherapy. But this much at least can be offered by way of a generalization: When those of us who are concerned

---

[6] *Babylonian Captivity*, Erl. Ed. op. var. arg., V, 82.

about people are *relatively* non-defensive about the positions we hold, not only will there be a possibility of achieving greater clarity in our formulations about our mutual disciplines, but we shall probably find much more basic agreement as to methods and goals than is now believed possible. To achieve such an end we who work in these fields must get to know one another and must share *ourselves* as well as our common concerns. For, as has been indicated, no matter whether we are therapists or theologians, what we are will determine what we do with others.

APPENDIX

CLINICAL TRAINING
In PREPARATION
For The PASTORAL MINISTRY

Clinical pastoral training, as we know it today, began with Dr. Anton T. Boisen at Worcester, Massachusetts, in the summer of 1924. There are some who question Dr. Boisen's right to be described as its founder, and he himself is too modest to claim the title, but I do not hesitate to ascribe it to him. To my knowledge, Dr. Boisen was the first clergyman to make special and clinical preparation before he undertook to become a mental hospital chaplain and to help others gain the understandings he achieved.

From the very beginning Dr. Boisen stressed the fact that real clinical learning could be achieved only through service. This was why he had his students work as ward attendants while obtaining clinical experience. Today we recognize that a theological student can make more of a contribution when he is allowed to be what he is: a student chaplain. Thus, he is not forced to occupy an unfamiliar role which is confusing both to the patient and to the student. Both student and patient gain most when the student is engaged in a *ministry of learning*.

We have found that the most meaningful ministry of learning comes about when the student seeks humbly to understand something of what the troubled person has experienced to make him as he is. The student does this by sharing himself—the greatest gift he has—himself, rooted and grounded in the Being of God. With this attitude in the student, the troubled person feels encouraged to reach out of the loneliness of his isolation for the help available. It is this attitude which is basic in any meaningful pastoral ministry. Clinical pastoral training provides the means whereby a supportive attitude, or its absence, can be detected; and the student is encouraged to develop his strengths and work through his deficiencies as he seeks to minister more helpfully to others.

From what has been said so far, a description of clinical pastoral training can be discerned. It could be put this way: Clinical pastoral training is a supervised experience which provides theological students and clergymen with opportunities for intensive clinical study of problems in the field of interpersonal relationships. It seeks to make clear to the student, in understanding and practice, the resources, methods and meanings of the Christian religion as they are expressed through pastoral care.

Thus, it becomes apparent that clinical experience is concerned with people *in crisis*; that is, people faced with the questions of ultimate, as well as immediate, concern: meaning, purpose, value, faith, hope and love—the soul's destiny. Such questions invariably occur in the sick-room where people often have no place to look but upwards. And, what is most important for us in clinical training, the student can find this an extraordinarily rich experience as, with the patient and guided by his supervisor, he struggles with fundamental issues of life and death.

Traditionally the word "clinical" implied learning or ministry at the *bedside* of the patient; hence we catch the original flavor of the meaning of *clinical baptism,* with all its rich potentiality. However, from the very beginning, Dr. Boisen tried to make clear that clinical pastoral training is a *process of learning* far more than a place in which the learning is carried out. Granted that a hospital or institution, with its controlled environment, is an ideal place to achieve clinical learning; it is not the only place. Indeed, I wish to suggest the following thesis: Adequate clinical pastoral training cannot begin apart from an institutional setting; but neither can adequate clinical preparation for the pastoral ministry be completed unless the training is supervised in a more normal, or parish, setting. This is not a new thought.[1]

What I predict for the future is a well-rounded program in which the student will achieve his basic orientation in the hospital

---

[1] It has been advocated at least since the spring of 1951 when I wrote an editorial in *The Journal of Pastoral Care* entitled "The Goals of Clinical Pastoral Training Re-appraised."

or institution setting; this experience will be fired and tested in the crucible of parish practice, under adequate supervision, *before* the candidate is finally ordained. For Anglicans I see this as an unparalleled opportunity to rethink and redesign the Diaconate so that it can come to be an apprenticeship as was originally intended.

Let us now return to this *process of learning* of which I spoke. What is meant is that in the hospital the chaplain as supervisor is willing and able to open himself and his operations to collaborative inquiry as he goes about the business of ministering to his patients. Here the chaplain supervisor allows his students to see how he operates in carrying out his functions. He is willing, as is appropriate, to discuss with his students what he has done, what he thinks about what he has done, how he feels about it, and what he would do if he could do it over again. The chaplain as supervisor or teacher seeks to help the student understand why he did or did not do something with the patient; what he hoped would come of his efforts; and in general gives his interpretation of the interpersonal situation in which he has been involved. He does this in such a way as to invite his students to ask questions, offer comments, and voice criticisms and doubts with a view toward facilitating interpersonal learning.

Such an emphasis on clinical learning covers vastly more than simply a *bedside*, person-to-person, or pastoral counseling relationship. This *process of learning* applies also to many other areas: for example, preaching, the sacramental and worship ministry, the tremendous resources and strengths found in sound doctrine and good practice. This last comes to be appreciated when, in regularly conducted religious discussion groups, the chaplain shows that his group work leadership is solidly grounded in the Scriptural understandings by which men have come to find life and death. These are the basic operations in which the chaplain, as chaplain, best serves his people in the time of crisis. These are the ministrations which provide rich and fruitful opportunity for students to sharpen their understandings as they go about their own ministry of learning.

This concept of *clinical* obviously necessitates dealing with the student-patient, student-teacher, student-pastor, and student-other-significant-persons relationships. Hence it is fundamental in present-day clinical pastoral training to help the student clarify the relationships which exist between himself and all others with whom he comes into vital contact. Thus, a rather fine distinction can be made: What we call clinical pastoral *education* is that process of *leading out* a student through the judicious use of a curriculum geared to enable him to grow, change and, certainly, to develop self-awareness. This is the goal of the seminary. Hence we get more light on a traditional emphasis in Anglican education: the aim of the first of three years is *purgative,* the second, *illuminative,* and the third, *unitive.* The hope, of course, is that in three years the student will have been transformed!

Clinical pastoral *training,* though it is involved in the process by which the student comes to be changed, cannot and should not make change in the student its major aim. It is the goal of the seminary to effect change in the student; it is the goal of the hospital, usually a secular institution, to provide him with the content of the clinical experience. That favorable change in a student's attitude will occur as a result of clinical confrontation, is a hoped-for consummation; but it can be only a by-product, not the direct aim, of training. In this sense we understand the Biblical axiom, "He that loseth his life shall find it." As the student loses himself in trying to understand the mentally ill patient, theories about mental illness and its treatment, problems related to the stigma and care of the mentally ill, and the relationship of various members of the helping professions to each other in the light of the minister's function and religious resources, constructive and durable change can and usually does occur in the student.

Clinical supervision, then, as we understand it, is the means of assisting a student to recognize and define *what* is going on and *how,* in his many and varied interpersonal relationships. However, to effect this there must be considerable development of self-awareness in the student. That this is rarely true for the student before he begins his clinical pastoral training has provoked some supervisors to attempt the impossible task of trying to be a therapist to the student, something for which the supervisor is not trained, and which is not his role. The student often does not recognize that he needs counseling, nor does he want it; he did not come to the hospital for treatment, but to get training. Hence, many a supervisor, unable to make the distinction between a student's counseling and training needs, finds himself in a pseudo-counseling relationship with his students which exhibits all the hallmarks of an exercise in futility. The day is now upon us when we can and must define more clearly the goals of supervision, and be able to distinguish between the students' counseling and training needs. Only by making these distinctions, clarifying our objectives in pretraining interviews and sharpening the goals of the program itself, can we hope to offer adequate clinical pastoral training.

From this understanding of clinical pastoral training we can see that it is one of the most significant resources a candidate has available for testing his vocation as a minister and his aptitude for counseling relationships. In the laboratory of interpersonal problems—the hospital—under competent supervision, the student can come to grips with what goes on between himself and other people. For as he exercises his ministry of learning, under the sensitive and skilled direction of a *chaplain* supervisor, so he comes to understand and accept his essential function as a minister of God.

All this presupposes that we can accept patients in mental hospitals as our teachers. For many this just is not so; these people prefer to look upon the mentally ill as those who should be ostracized and isolated from the rest of the community.

I am reminded of those patients who had descended into the hell of despair, and in their anguish cried out *against* God—"My God, my God! *Why?*" And He heard them. They were not rebuked—as Jonah was not rebuked when he cried to the Almighty, "I do well to be angry!" Indeed, they were delivered, and their means of deliverance was the honest, open and often violent sharing of feelings with which we all have trouble.

One of our patients was a very sick woman, who had just taken a major step toward recovery when her husband was shot in a liquor store holdup. The next day, when visiting hours came, she looked for her husband to bring her the coat which she was planning to wear to church. Instead, she was visited by police officers who told her of his death. The psychiatrist, fearing a return to the bizarre schizophrenic behavior into which she had earlier retreated, and knowing of her positive interest in religion, referred her to the chaplain. She was seen immediately, encouraged to talk about her victimized husband, and helped to ventilate some of her guilts about their life together. At first she denied the reality of his death, so great was the shock; and she was not pressed to accept it. By the third interview she was ready to share a terrifying dream which helped her admit the reality of death and her own fears and resentments about this death, which she had in some measure anticipated from the life she knew her husband had been living. All this of course did not come about without tears and the expression of strong feeling. Then it became clear again: "Blessed are those who mourn, for they shall be comforted." This patient did not relapse into her former schizo-phrenic state, and not too long after this episode recovered sufficiently to be discharged from the hospital. The chaplain saw her a total of three or four times over a period of eight days. Such a ministry rarely comes about except where the chaplain is prepared both by extensive hospital experience and specialized clinical pastoral training.

To quote Dr. Boisen again: The hospital can provide what the classroom lacks, opportunities for confrontation with "the living human document" which demonstrates "sin and salvation in flesh and blood." The clinical situation provides the experiences which present the questions for which Christian theology has the answers. But too often we have rushed in with answers before there were any ques-tions, and of course have not been heard. There is no better place than a mental hospital to make clear the futility of such an attempt.

Today we find many who are asking the basic questions with which life confronts us all. Many are demanding answers that can only come out of the realm of faith and religion. Who among us can say that the Church, with its rich heritage of faith and practice, is speaking relevantly to the age in which we live? Yet it is given to the Church to provide the leadership whereby men can find the meaning and purpose, communion and commitment, that are req-uisite for "the soul's health." With bitter satire, however, Dr. Hobart Mowrer points up the dilemma in which many of us find ourselves. He said he had deliberately forsaken the Church and religion, but, years later, "When I wanted to come home, I found nobody at home."

Ours is a time when we need to learn again the ancient wisdom that portrayed theology as the "Queen of the Sciences." For it is only when we have an adequate theology, relevantly applied to the issues at hand, and shared rather than forced upon people, that we can find the light that illumines and the seed which can give new life. Then we can see religion as religion must be seen to give life: a dimension in all functions which gives meaning and purpose to human existence.

That this can happen we have found true with our hospital patients. When the essential "good news" of God's forgiveness and understanding are intelligently and sensitively shared with patients, we have often found that the shackles of misunderstanding, fear, ignorance, suspicion, hate and even tender feelings which have been denied, can be struck off and the captives made free. Then we are proclaiming "the acceptable year of the Lord." It is our high calling so to represent Him who is the Way, the Truth and the Life, that the Word may become flesh and dwell among us. It will not be surprising then to hear that some have come to see "the goodness of the Lord in the land of the living." This at least is what we hold up to our students as the great need and our opportunity through a ministry of learning in clinical pastoral training.

So far, I have argued for clinical training in the hospital. It has been my thesis that adequate pastoral preparation cannot be made without the hospital experience; but neither is the hospital experience to be regarded as all that is necessary for such preparation. Unfortunately for many this has not yet become clear; hence for many seminarians and some seminaries the only clinical preparation is that obtained in the hospital. Small wonder that there is growing criticism of clinical training, suspicion about it, and in some instances a withdrawal from it.

What we need today is the integration of the clinical emphasis into the theological curriculum. Only when this is done will we see the establishment of adequate parish-centered clinical pastoral training. The following is suggested as a possible means of obtaining good clinical orientation in the hospital while at the same time making sure that such training is not merely added to an existing theological curriculum.

I would envisage that the seminarian, in his first year at

seminary, would be given two major opportunities to prepare him for his clinical orientation. The first would be a one-semester, three-hour course in pastoral psychology taught by a clinically trained theological professor. This would give the student the basic data and language of dynamic principles in personality development, mental mechanisms and an understanding of some of the fundamentals of depth psychology as these illuminate the pastoral office. In conjunction with this course, for one hour each week during both semesters, the student would meet his classmates in a small group (seven is preferred). Here the aims are to take the raw data of the student's need to make new friends, his questions and perplexities about his new venture in life (studying for the Christian ministry) and his concerns about the seminary, and allow them free expression. In such an unstructured group experience, under the guidance of a clinically trained leader sensitive to group dynamics, a by-product must inevitably be the development of self-awareness within the student. With such a program behind him in the first year, along with the other theological training he would have received, he would come to the hospital equipped with basic knowledge and sufficient self-awareness to make the most of his first experience in clinical pastoral training.

I recommend that one full day a week during both semesters of the middle year be spent in hospital clinical pastoral training in a carefully structured program. The day would begin with his participation in a daily 15-minute meditation service held regularly for patients and staff. Next would come an hour-and-a-half lecture-seminar conducted by a staff member, a chaplain supervisor, or a second-year chaplain resident in training. This seminar would present some of the essential data about mentally ill patients, mental illness and its problems and treatment, the hospital and its community relationships and the chaplain's program, delineating the religious resources used in ministering to the mentally ill as the chaplain works with other members of "the healing team."

Next the student would have at least two hours visiting with patients in the wards as his introduction to clinical pastoral experience. Such visits, even though unstructured, provide the material which the student would write up for critical evaluation with his supervisor. During the day each student would have approximately one hour for supervisory consultation. The day would finish with an hour-and-a-half "group concerns seminar" under competent group leadership, to give the student opportunity to verbalize his understanding and/or perplexities about what he has heard, seen, read and felt during that day, and since the last day he was in the hospital. The student would be required to submit a weekly evaluation report of his total experiences sufficiently in advance of each week's session so that his supervisor would be ready to discuss intelligently with him the progress he is making.

In conjunction with his hospital experience, it would be necessary to have one two-hour seminar each week at the seminary, led by a professor who would raise theological concerns to which the students could present the relevant clinical data. Such a seminar would be held in the second semester, and professors from the various departments of the seminary's curriculum would participate. Of course it is hoped that these professors would themselves have undertaken such clinical training in order to be familiar with what the students are experiencing.

If such a program could be worked out in close collaboration with a hospital that had sufficient training resources, the student should be clinically well oriented by the end of his second year. Such students would then be prepared to spend at least six months, and preferably a full year, before their final year in seminary in a closely supervised parish program. Under such a program, ministers graduating from seminary could speak more relevantly to the deeper needs of people.

Some may wonder why a one-day-a-week, two-semester course is substituted for the current three-month full-time program usually given during the summer. The problems involved for a seminarian in being free during the summer months make such training impossible for a large number. In addition, there is the criticism that such summer training is never really "in course," and has resulted in clinical pastoral training's becoming largely just another course in the theological curriculum. The recommended program has two major values. The first is that throughout his second year, the student is confronted by clinical concerns in the hospital one day a week, and is required to struggle with the theological answers during the rest of the week. The seminar during the second semester at the seminary will aid materially in this direction.

In the second place, clinical work spread over a full year will generate far less anxiety then we usually find in students during the summer courses. In the one-day-a-week course, the mobilized anxiety can be helpfully directed, since it is spread over the whole week. The summer student's anxieties often result in seriously inhibiting his productivity unless the supervisor offers heroic compensatory measures.

There is, of course, a real place for the present three-month summer courses. My experience at Saint Elizabeths Hospital leads me to believe that perhaps six weeks, certainly ten weeks full-time, is all the time needed to effect the helpful kind of clinical training that seminaries desire at this time. Such three-month courses will always be needed by seminaries too far away from clinical centers or otherwise unable to have the students taking their training "in course."

The summer courses offer unusual opportunities to those outstanding students who show special promise in working more closely with people. With such a program here presented, the outstanding students in clinical work during their middle year could take the more intensive summer courses. These students, on returning to seminary in their senior year, would be excellent candidates to give supervised leadership in the orientation seminars previously described. Such orientation courses could then be offered for two full years of seminary education. In addition, they would give superior candidates additional supervised opportunities in experience-centered activities with people.

Obviously, part of what has just been outlined is in the planning stage. But what should be emphasized is that most of what is being reported here is the product of nearly 20 years' experience in an outstanding clinical training center. Today we can move much more rapidly and with much greater assurance than ever before.[2]

---

[2] A brief word should be said about postgraduate education. Wesley Theological Seminary in Washington, D.C., is already offering a master's program in Pastoral Theology in conjunction with the two-year full-time chaplain resident program at Saint Elizabeths Hospital. This is the only known

APPENDIX

Move we must if we are going to minister to the urgent demands
of people's needs. In *Action for Mental Health*, Report of the Joint
Commission on Mental Illness and Health, 1961, we are told that
42 per cent of all people seeking help with their difficulties in living
turn first to a clergyman. That report encourages our profession to
do more at both the preventive and therapeutic levels. For this we
must be more adequately trained than is yet possible in most of our
seminaries. Clinical pastoral training programs are a major step in
supplying such a need. The advances being made in some clinical
pastoral programs augur well for the adequate training of men for
the pastoral ministry.

program with such clinical pastoral training demands. On the drawing board
are plans to expand this to include a doctoral program. The basic aim of the
program is to enable superior students to take at least forty hours each week of
clinical training for two years. But along with this, stretching over a period
of three years, the student is encouraged to raise the relevant theological issues
and critically explore these issues under competent theological supervision at
graduate seminary level, so that at least one of the issues can be delimited to
provide a master's or doctoral thesis. The doctoral program is not envisaged as
being completed in less than five years. Only candidates of superior potential in
the pastoral field, with demonstrated pastoral competence following seminary
graduation, will be encouraged.

BIBLIOGRAPHY

INTRODUCTORY

ENGEL, LEONARD. *New Trends in the Care and Treatment of the Mentally Ill.* New York: National Association for Mental Health, 1959.

HART, BERNARD. *The Psychology of Insanity.* New York: Macmillan Co., 1931.

(Report of the) Joint Commission on Mental Health and Illness, *Action for Mental Health.* New York: Basic Books, 1961.

KLINK, THOMAS W. *Clergyman's Guide to Recognizing Serious Mental Illness.* New York: The National Association for Mental Health (pamphlet).

McCANN, RICHARD. *The Churches and Mental Health.* New York: Basic Books, 1962.

MILT, HARRY. *Basic Facts About Mental Illness.* New York: Scientific Aids Publications, 1959.

PRESTON, GEORGE H. *Psychiatry for the Curious.* New York: Holt, Rinehart and Winston, Inc., 1940.

PRESTON, GEORGE H. *The Substance of Mental Health.* New York: Holt, Rinehart and Winston, Inc., 1943.

HISTORICAL

BEERS, CLIFFORD. *A Mind That Found Itself.* New York: Doubleday & Co., Inc., 1960.

BOISEN, ANTON T. *Exploration of the Inner World.* Chicago: Willett, Clark & Co., 1936.

BOISEN, ANTON T. *Religion in Crisis and Custom.* New York: Harper & Row, Publishers, 1955.

135

BRILL, A. A. *Basic Writings of Sigmund Freud.* New York: Random House, 1938.

DEUTSCH, ALBERT. *A History of the Mentally Ill in America.* New York: Columbia University Press, 1950.

JAMES, WILLIAM. *Varieties of Religious Experience.* New York: Random House, 1929.

MUNROE, RUTH L. *Schools of Psychoanalytic Thought.* New York: Dryden Press, 1955.

RAY, MARIE BENYON. *Doctors of the Mind.* Boston: Little, Brown & Co., 1944.

THOMPSON, CLARA. *Psychoanalysis: Evolution and Development.* New York: Hermitage House, 1950.

OF SELF AND CHARACTER

DE FOREST, IZETTE. *The Leaven of Love.* New York: Harper & Row, Publishers, 1954.

ENGLISH, O. SPURGEON, and GERALD H. J. PEARSON, *Emotional Problems of Living.* New York: W. W. Norton & Co., 1955.

FENICHEL, OTTO. *The Psychoanalytic Theory of Neurosis.* New York: W. W. Norton & Co., 1945.

FOSDICK, HARRY EMERSON. *On Being a Real Person.* New York: Harper & Row, Publishers, 1943.

FREUD, ANNA. *The Ego and Mechanisms of Defense.* New York: International Universities Press, 1946.

FROMM, ERICH. *Man for Himself.* New York: Holt, Rinehart and Winston, Inc., 1947.

HORNEY, KAREN. *The Neurotic Personality of Our Time.* New York: W. W. Norton & Co., 1937.

MAY, ROLLO. *Man's Search for Himself.* New York: W. W. Norton & Co., 1953.

MAY, ROLLO. *The Meaning of Anxiety.* New York: Ronald Press, 1950.

MULLAHY, PAT. *Oedipus—Myth and Complex.* New York: Hermitage House, 1948.

RIBBLE, MARGARET A. *The Rights of Infants.* New York: Columbia University Press, 1943.

RIESMAN, DAVID, NATHAN GLAZER and REUEL DENNEY. *The Lonely Crowd.* New Haven: Yale University Press, 1953.

SAUL, L. J. *Emotional Maturity.* New York: J. B. Lippincott, 1947.

Sullivan, Harry S. *The Interpersonal Theory of Psychiatry*. New York: W. W. Norton & Co., 1953.

Suttie, Ian D. and Paul Kogan. *The Origins of Love and Hate*. London: Trench, Trubner Ltd., 1935.

Tournier, Paul. *Escape from Loneliness*. Philadelphia: Westminster Press, 1962.

Tournier, Paul. *The Meaning of Persons*. New York: Harper & Row, Publishers, Inc., 1957.

MENTAL ILLNESS

American Handbook of Psychiatry, Vol. 1, Part 3, Sections 23–26. New York: Basic Books, 1959.

American Handbook of Psychiatry, Vol. 2, Parts 9 & 10. New York: Basic Books, 1959.

Beers, Clifford. *A Mind That Found Itself*. New York: Longmans & Co., 1908.

Boisen—*

Fromm-Reichmann, Frieda. *Principles of Intensive Psychotherapy*. Chicago: University of Chicago Press, 1950.

Fromm-Reichmann, Frieda. *Psychoanalysis and Psychotherapy* (Selected Papers). Chicago: University of Chicago Press, 1959.

Maslow, A. H., and Bela Mittelmann. *Principles of Abnormal Psychology*. New York: Harper & Row, Publishers, 1951.

Menninger, Karl. *Theory of Psychoanalytic Technique*. New York: Basic Books, 1958.

Noyes, Arthur P., and Lawrence C. Kolb. *Modern Clinical Psychiatry*. Philadelphia: W. B. Saunders Co., 1958.

Oates, Wayne E. *Religious Factors in Mental Illness*. New York: Association Press, 1955.

Overholser, Winfred. *Handbook of Psychiatry*. Philadelphia: J. B. Lippincott, 1947.

Reik, Theodore. *Listening with the Third Ear*. New York: Farrar, Straus and Cudahy, Inc., 1954.

Stern, Edith. *Mental Illness: A Guide for the Family*. New York: Harper & Row, Publishers, 1962.

Tabor, Eithne. *The Cliff's Edge*. New York: Sheed & Ward, 1950.

* See section—"Historical"

WISE, CARROLL. *Religion in Illness and Health*. New York: Harper & Row, Publishers, 1942.

PASTORAL CARE AND COUNSELING

CABOT, RICHARD C., and RUSSELL L. DICKS. *The Art of Ministering to the Sick*. New York: Macmillan Co., 1944.

DICKS, RUSSELL L. *Pastoral Work and Personal Counseling*. New York: Macmillan Co., 1949.

DUNBAR, H. FLANDERS. *Mind and Body*. New York: Emerson Books, 1937.

HILTNER, SEWARD. *Pastoral Counseling*. Nashville: Abingdon Press, 1949.

JACKSON, EDGAR N. *Understanding Grief*. Nashville: Abingdon Press, 1957.

LEVINE, MAURICE. *Psychotherapy in Medical Practice*. New York: Macmillan Co., 1947.

MAY, ROLLO. *The Art of Counseling*. Nashville: Abingdon Press, 1939.

McNEILL, JOHN T. *The History of the Cure of Souls*. New York: Harper & Row, Publishers, 1951.

OATES, WAYNE E. *The Bible in Pastoral Care*. Philadelphia: Westminster Press, 1953.

OATES, WAYNE E. *The Christian Pastor*. Philadelphia: Westminster Press, 1951.

SPANN, J. RICHARD. *Pastoral Care*. Nashville: Abingdon Press, 1951.

STEINER, LEE R. *Where Do People Take Their Troubles?* Boston: Houghton Mifflin Co., 1945.

SULLIVAN, HARRY S. *The Psychiatric Interview*. New York: W. W. Norton & Co., 1954.

WEISS, EDWARD, and O. SPURGEON ENGLISH. *Psychosomatic Medicine*. Philadelphia: W. B. Saunders Co., 1943.

WISE, CARROLL A. *Pastoral Counseling*. New York: Harper & Row, Publishers, 1951.

RELIGION AND PSYCHIATRY

BONTHIUS, ROBERT H. *Christian Paths to Self Acceptance*. New York: King's Crown Press, 1954.

COLE, WILLIAM GRAHAM. *Sex in Christianity and Psychoanalysis.* New York: Oxford University Press, 1955.

DONIGER, SIMON (ED.). *Healing: Human and Divine.* New York: Association Press, 1957.

FREUD, SIGMUND. *The Future of an Illusion.* New York: Liverwright Publishing Corp., 1949.

FROMM, ERICH. *Psychoanalysis and Religion.* New Haven: Yale University Press, 1950.

HOWE, REUEL. *Man's Need and God's Action.* Greenwich, Connecticut: The Seabury Press, 1953.

MAVES, PAUL B. *The Church and Mental Health.* New York: Charles Scribner's Sons, 1953.

MAVES, P. B., and J. L. CEDARLEAF. *Older People and the Church.* Nashville: Abingdon Press, 1949.

ROBERTS, DAVID E. *Psychotherapy and a Christian View of Man.* New York: Charles Scribner's Sons, 1950.

TILLICH, PAUL. *The Courage to Be.* New Haven: Yale University Press, 1952.

TILLICH, PAUL. *The New Being.* New York: Charles Scribner's Sons, 1955.

THE INFANT AND YOUNG CHILD

BRUCH, HILDE. *Don't Be Afraid of Your Child.* New York: Farrar, Straus and Cudahy, Inc., 1952.

Child Study Association of America. *Parents' Questions and Helpful Answers.* New York: Harper & Row, Publishers, 1947.

FREUD, ANNA. *Psychoanalysis for Teachers and Parents.* New York: Emerson Books, 1935.

SPOCK, BENJAMIN. *Common-Sense Book of Baby and Child Care.* New York: Pocket Books, Inc., 1947.

MARITAL AND SEXUAL ADJUSTMENT

BERGLER, EDMUND. *Conflict in Marriage.* New York: Harper & Row, Publishers, 1949.

BUTTERFIELD, O. M. *Sex Life in Marriage.* New York: Emerson Books, 1937.

Cuber, J. F. *Marriage Counseling Practice*. New York: Appleton-Century-Crofts, Inc., 1948.

Doniger, Simon. *Sex and Religion Today*. New York: Association Press, 1953.

Duvall, S. M. *Before You Marry*. New York: Association Press, 1949.

Duvall, S. M., and R. Hill. *When You Marry*. New York: Association Press, 1953.

Lewin, S. A., and J. Gilmore. *Sex Without Fear*. New York: Lear Publishers, 1950.

PHYSICAL ILLNESS

Dicks, Russell L. *Who Is My Patient?* New York: Macmillan Co., 1941.

Standard, S. and H. Nathan. *Should the Patient Know the Truth?* New York: Springer Publishing Co., 1955.

of GENERAL INTEREST

Alcoholics Anonymous (revised). New York: Alcoholics Anonymous Publishing Co., 1955.

Allport, G. *The Individual and His Religion*. New York: Macmillan Co., 1950.

Bergler, Edmund. *Divorce Won't Help*. New York: Harper & Row, Publishers, 1948.

Boisen, Anton T. *Out of the Depths*. New York: Harper & Row, Publishers, 1960.

Bullis, H. E. *Human Relations in the Classroom*. Wilmington: Delaware State Society for Mental Hygiene, 1904.

Clinebell, Howard J., Jr. *Understanding and Counseling the Alcoholic*. Nashville: Abingdon Press, 1956.

Dahl, Robert. *Breakdown*. New York: Bobbs-Merrill Co., 1959.

Fletcher, Joseph. *Morals and Medicine*. Princeton: Princeton University Press, 1954.

Freeman, Lucy. *Fight against Fears*. New York: Crown Publishers, 1951.

FROMM, ERICH. *Man for Himself*. New York: Holt, Rinehart and Winston, Inc., 1947.

FROMM, ERICH. *The Sane Society*. New York: Holt, Rinehart and Winston, Inc., 1955.

KEGLEY, CHARLES W., and ROBERT W. BRETALL. *The Theology of Paul Tillich*. New York: Macmillan Co., 1952.

KIERKEGAARD, SØREN. *The Concept of Dread* (translated by Walter Lowrie). Princeton: Princeton University Press, 1946.

KIERKEGAARD, SØREN. *Sickness Unto Death* (translated by Walter Lowrie). Princeton: Princeton University Press, 1946.

LINN, LOUIS. *Psychiatry and Religious Experience*. New York: Random House, 1958.

MACCASLAND, S. V. *By the Finger of God*. New York: Macmillan Co., 1951.

MOORE, BRIAN. *The Lonely Passion of Judith Hearne*. Boston: Atlantic—Little, Brown and Company, 1956.

NIEBUHR, H. R., D. D. WILLIAMS and J. M. GUSTAFSON. *The Advancement of Theological Education*. New York: Harper & Row, Publishers, 1957.

NIEBUHR, REINHOLD. *The Nature and Destiny of Man*. New York: Charles Scribner's Sons, 1941.

OVERSTREET, BONARO. *Understanding Fear in Ourselves and Others*. New York: Harper & Row, Publishers, 1951.

ROGERS, W. F. *Ye Shall Be Comforted*. Philadelphia: Westminster Press, 1950.

SYKES, GERALD. *The Hidden Remnant*. New York: Harper & Row, Publishers, 1962.

VAN VELDE, JACOBA. *The Big Ward*. New York: Simon & Schuster, 1960.

WARD, ARCHIBALD F., JR. *Seasons of the Soul*. Richmond, Virginia: John Knox Press, 1960.

Where to Turn. Health & Welfare Council of the National Capital Area, Washington, D.C.

JOURNALS

The Journal of Pastoral Care. Published by the Council for Clinical Training and the Institute for Pastoral Care, New York City.

Journal of Religion and Health. Published by the Academy of Religion and Mental Health, New York City.

Pastoral Psychology. Published by Pastoral Psychology Press, Manhasset, N.Y.

Psychiatry: Journal for the Study of Interpersonal Processes. Published by the William A. White Psychiatric Foundation, Washington, D.C.

INDEX

143